THE LIGHT IN OUR ⊏ᴛ⊏ᴜ

"The numbers do not lie. A remarkable amount of those under the age of forty have become disillusioned with the evangelical 'bully' subculture in America. Nicholas McDonald not only tries to understand this reality but also provides an alternative way to address it. In a rare spirit of sympathy with the criticisms (and healthy bit of humor), McDonald makes a compelling case that replacing a joyless Christianity with a joyless deconstruction is a dead end. The path to recovery begins by being disillusioned with disillusionment, finding a road to more joy (not less) and thereby finding one's way back to the genuine Jesus. This is a desperately needed book."

—RICHARD LINTS, senior advisor of Redeemer City
to City (NYC) and senior professor of theology
at Gordon-Conwell Theological Seminary

"In *The Light in Our Eyes,* McDonald invites us to reclaim a vision of Christian faith that isn't bound on either side by argumentation and contemporary political positions. This charming, insightful, and funny book casts a vision for faith that is, in fact, quite ancient. This narrative is for those who are weary of a Christianity that has become a collection of position papers and who hunger to re-remember the dreams of Jesus."

—JOHN HENDRIX, *New York Times* bestselling author/
illustrator of *The Mythmakers: The Remarkable
Fellowship of C.S. Lewis and J.R.R. Tolkien*

"Many people are disillusioned by what they believe to be Christianity but what is, in fact, a false narrative that McDonald calls 'the story of escape.' In reality, Christianity is a wondrous drama of rootedness and renewal, and this book invites readers to be 're-storied' and to embrace faith in Jesus with a restored imagination. The church may have many cracks, but—to riff off a song by Leonard Cohen—sometimes that's how the light gets in, guiding us back to the beauty of God. With this book, McDonald rings the bell that still can ring and beckons us to listen and look."

—WESLEY VANDER LUGT, theologian and author of
Beauty Is Oxygen: Finding a Faith That Breathes

"This book couldn't be more timely. Nicholas McDonald understands from personal experience the currents that have led countless individuals to deconstruct their faith and embrace 'exvangelicalism.' Drawing on his personal journey and voices as varied as Kermit or Tim Burton, Nick Cave or The Beatles, Tolstoy, Augustine, and especially C. S. Lewis, he finds the antidote to today's disillusionment. For the church's flawed—occasionally even toxic or bullying—witness, McDonald offers an understandable response to her hypocrisy, tribalism, and abuses. He invites us to discover that Jesus's gospel and dream for the world offers us hope and love in richer and more life-enhancing ways than we could ever imagine. This helpful and encouraging book will provide much-needed water to many lost in the desert."

—MARK MEYNELL, writer, pastor, and mentor, formerly
Europe and Caribbean director for Langham Preaching,
and author of several books including *A Wilderness
of Mirrors* and co-editor of *Not So with You:
Power and Leadership for the Church*

"*The Light in Our Eyes* offers those struggling with doubt, disillusionment, and deconstruction the room to name and acknowledge what is legitimately troubling within contemporary evangelical Christianity, while encouraging a more ancient, global, and hope-filled vision of the Christian faith. Drawing from his journey of deconstruction and restoration, as well as the questions and experiences of students he has mentored, McDonald invites readers to set aside shallow or incomplete understandings of faith in favor of a richer biblical vision. I expect this gracious and appropriately critical book will help many rediscover Jesus and recover a living, dynamic relationship with Him."

—MARK P. RYAN, executive director of Sage Christianity and associate professor of congregational theology and cultural apologetics at Calvin Theological Seminary—Missional Training Center

THE
LIGHT
IN OUR
EYES

THE
LIGHT
IN OUR
EYES

Rediscovering the Love, Beauty, and Freedom
of Jesus in an Age of Disillusionment

Nicholas McDonald

Foreword by Karen Swallow Prior

MULTNOMAH

Multnomah
An imprint of the Penguin Random House Christian Publishing Group,
a division of Penguin Random House LLC
1745 Broadway, New York, NY 10019
waterbrookmultnomah.com
penguinrandomhouse.com

This is a work of nonfiction. Some names and identifying details have been changed.

Italics in Scripture quotations reflect the author's added emphasis.

A Multnomah Trade Paperback Original

Library of Congress Cataloging-in-Publication Data
Names: McDonald, Nicholas (Pastor), author.
Title: The light in our eyes: rediscovering the love, beauty, and freedom of Jesus in an age of disillusionment / Nicholas McDonald.
Description: [Colorado Springs, CO] : Multnomah, [2025] | Includes bibliographical references.
Identifiers: LCCN 2024043185 | ISBN 9780593601525 (trade paperback) | ISBN 9780593601532 (ebook)
Subjects: LCSH: Christian life—Presbyterian authors.
Classification: LCC BV4501.3 .M3325 2025 | DDC 248.4—dc23/eng/20241211
LC record available at https://lccn.loc.gov/2024043185

Printed in the United States of America on acid-free paper

1st Printing

The authorized representative in the EU for product safety and compliance is Penguin Random House Ireland, Morrison Chambers, 32 Nassau Street, Dublin D02 YH68, Ireland, https://eu-contact.penguin.ie.

BOOK TEAM: Production editor: Helen Macdonald • Managing editor: Julia Wallace • Production manager: Ali Wagner • Copy editor: Rachel Kirsch • Proofreaders: Tracey Moore, Carrie Krause, Drew Goter

Book design by Caroline Cunningham
Sunburst: mayrum/Adobe Stock; emoticons: Pure Imagination/Adobe Stock; arrow: Saepol/ Adobe Stock; triangle: line's vector/Adobe Stock; crown: 4zevar/Adobe Stock

For details on special quantity discounts for bulk purchases, contact specialmarketscms@penguinrandomhouse.com.

Foreword

There can be no doubt that the American church—particularly the evangelical church—is facing a mounting crisis. As documented in the pages of this book, the number of evangelicals who can now be described as dechurched, deconstructed, or having departed from their truth is rising dramatically.

One writer depicted such a moment in the church:

Ordinary Christians came to have greater expectations of what the church ought to be doing. When expectations weren't met, people began to criticize the church in all kinds of ways. One of the things you see developing is a real cynicism on the part of ordinary Christians about the church and the clergy.[1]

Notably, these words weren't written to describe our current church situation. Rather, they were penned decades ago by theologian and historian Alister McGrath. McGrath was writing about a period in the church that took place hundreds of years ago, during the time leading up to the Protestant Reformation. Yet McGrath's words sound eerily familiar, don't they? Here is more from the article: "The late Middle Ages saw the church going through a period of real doctrinal confusion. People were not sure what they believed. They weren't sure why they believed it, either."[2]

It was truly a time of crisis for the church. Yet that crisis, mercifully, led to much needed change through both the Reformation and the Counter-Reformation that followed. As McGrath put it,

> By looking at the way God restored, renewed and reformed his church back then, we can gain some ideas about what he might want to do to his church here, today, in this place. It is about looking through history to discover what God has been doing in the past, then we can say, "Maybe he wants to do that kind of thing here today."[3]

What American evangelicalism is going through now can, just as it has in the past, lead to renewal, refinement, and even reformation. I believe this deeply—not just despite but even because of the disillusionment within and toward the church we see today.

Let's consider the current movement of protest within the church called "Deconstruction."

When the word *deconstruction* gained currency among Christians a few years ago—particularly among younger and evangelical believers—many in the church were alarmed. To be sure, a certain amount of alarm was (and is) warranted. The fact is that some of the first and the loudest of those who were "deconstructing their faith" walked away from the church and Christianity altogether. It seemed that deconstruction (whatever that is, since the definition of the word itself has been contested and continues to be used in a variety of ways) would always lead inevitably to unbelief.

But that seeming inevitability has been shown not to be the case. In fact, I see more cause for hope than alarm through this trend toward deconstruction. If you don't agree with me, wait until you finish reading *The Light in Our Eyes*. I think you will see what I mean. I think you will find much reason to hope in the midst of this transitional period in the church—whether you are someone watching others deconstruct or you are someone undergoing that process yourself.

It might be helpful to think through the word *deconstruction* for the metaphor it is.

It does not mean "destroy" or "destruct" (although, sadly, that might sometimes be the ultimate outcome). Rather, *deconstruction* suggests taking apart something that has been constructed. Something that has been built up over time, added to, covered, exposed, walled up, papered over, dusted, decorated, and perhaps decayed. Like buildings, our very lives are constructed over time through events, relationships, and experiences that accumulate, layer upon layer. So, too, our faith—which begins with the simple belief in Jesus as Savior and Lord—can accumulate complicated apparatuses built up over time.

Just as buildings sometimes require examination to see what parts are solid and necessary and what are merely extraneous or even rotten or dangerous, so too, the components of our faith require such examination. Deconstruction isn't just asking questions. And it's not just a look at the surface level of things. It's taking something apart and examining it from the foundation up.

This means, of course, it's a process laden with risk. That's what makes it necessary to come alongside those involved in this hard, painful, and often scary work of examining the once-unexamined assumptions of evangelical culture. (Or to come alongside others if we are the ones doing this work.)

What other choice do we have? As Nicholas shows in the pages that follow, people are disillusioned, doubting, leaving the church, and departing from Christianity—not just deconstructing. But coming alongside those who are disillusioned, doubting, or departing isn't something we should do just as a reactionary measure because we fear change or don't want decline in influence or power. Rather, we do this holy work because it is part of being faithful in the times to which God has called us.

After all, as Nicholas shows so compellingly and beautifully in this book, Jesus came to restore each of us to a right relationship with our Creator, with creation, and with one another. Too many in the modern church and the surrounding culture don't know this. Or, perhaps, in the storm and stress of life, we have forgotten it. We don't see it. So we don't even desire it. To help others see such good, we must see it too. To help others desire it, we must desire it ourselves.

Jesus wants all the rotten boards to be removed, the crooked beams to be made straight, the floors to be made level, and the windows to be cleaned to let the light shine in. The church is His house, and He has made His house to be a place of peace, love, beauty, and freedom. These are the things that put the light in our eyes. And in the world.

When I read the words of a younger believer like Nicholas McDonald—the words of someone who has doubted, questioned, asked, listened, seen, heard, and proven to be faithful—I see more light ahead in the church and the world. I think in reading these pages, you will too.

—KAREN SWALLOW PRIOR

Contents

PART 3 Jesus's Dreams

THE
LIGHT
IN OUR
EYES

1

Disillusionment, Deconstruction, and the Great Dechurching

To make our way forward is to go back in history. To recover past trauma is to awaken to the pain, and we cannot heal until we see the narratives of the past renewed by faith and hope. We cannot move forward by ignoring the past.
—MAKOTO FUJIMURA, *Silence and Beauty*

Can faith be bought
in supermarkets
Like canned soup
lined up in a row?
If it is defective
may I return it?
As it is two sizes
too small.
—E R SKULMOSKI, "Both the Wicked and the
Righteous Have a Midlife Crisis"

You probably know this by now, and if you don't, it's time: The American evangelical church is facing the largest mass exodus ever recorded. It would not be an exaggeration to say that tens of millions of people have left the church over the past decade. You might be one of them.

In their book *The Great Dechurching,* Jim Davis and Michael Graham observed,

> More people have left the church in the last twenty-five years than all the new people who became Christians from the First Great Awakening, Second Great Awakening, and Billy Graham crusades *combined.* Adding to the alarm is the fact that this phenomenon has rapidly increased since the mid-1990s.[1]

Those who've dechurched often call their experience "deconstruction." The term has grown in popularity thanks to trending #exvangelical social media influencers like Joshua Harris, Abraham Piper, and Rhett and Link. But *deconstruction* is often a slippery term to define. Is everyone who has dechurched also deconstructed? Is everyone who is deconstructing also dechurching? Is there such a thing as "good deconstruction"? Hip-hop artist Lecrae has suggested that, yes, deconstruction *can* be a good thing:

> Many don't realize there have been healthy Deconstructions throughout history. . . . There are generations of believers who have been thru this and we can learn from them versus destroying our life and faith trying to figure it out alone. . . . Many movements from the reformation to the civil rights movement involved deconstruction using scripture and then reconstruction. I offer this as an encouragement to those struggling. My faith is stronger than ever. I've been there and healing is possible.[2]

Others like Alisa Childers and Tim Barnett have taken issue with this, saying, "Faith deconstruction is a postmodern process of rethinking your faith without regarding Scripture as a standard," so faithful Christians should not use this term to describe healthy spiritual growth.[3] But is the characterization of deconstruction as a full-throated rejection of Scripture fair or accurate? That may be true of the loudest online voices of the deconstruction movement. But Davis and Graham observed that, on the whole, the dechurched tend not to be critical of orthodoxy:

> Dechurched evangelicals are still largely orthodox in their faith. When it comes to our primary doctrines, 68 percent of those we surveyed still believe in the Trinity, 64 percent believe in the divinity of Jesus, 65 percent believe Jesus' death on the cross paid the penalty for the sins of those who believe in him, 67 percent believe in the resurrection, 62 percent believe that Jesus is the only way to God, and 61 percent believe the Bible is a reliable document for all matters of faith and practice.[4]

This would strongly suggest that the term *deconstruction* is not a one-size-fits-all description. In my experience, folks mean at least four separate—but related—things when they use the term *deconstructing* to describe themselves. That's why a better approach would be to see deconstruction as a spectrum of postures.

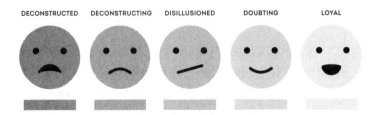

DECONSTRUCTED   DECONSTRUCTING   DISILLUSIONED   DOUBTING   LOYAL

1. THE LOYAL

The Loyal would not use *deconstructing* to describe themselves, because they tend not to question the cultural assumptions of American Evangelicalism (more on that term in a moment). They feel happy and at home in the evangelical church and assume the deconstruction movement is coming from progressive influences on the next generation. There are plenty of faithful evangelical Loyals whom I know and love. Those in this category likely find it very difficult to be helpful to their children, nieces and nephews, or grandchildren unless they have some clear grasp of why their loved ones are deconstructing in the first place. My hope is that this book provides the Loyal some context for a conversation and hopefully makes the whole thing sound less frightening. If you are in the Loyal camp, many things in this book may make you feel guarded. That's understandable. But I encourage you to read through the whole text before coming to a conclusion, because in order to reach your deconstructing friends and loved ones, you're going to need to sit in these uncomfortable spaces with patience and respect. Jumping to hasty conclusions or using quick labels is the surest way to alienate them. For example, in this book I will speak candidly about how American Evangelicals have tied Christian faithfulness to certain political ideologies. But the truth is, I'm embarrassingly elastic and I'd like to think somewhat eclectic in my political opinions.

I know and admire faithful Christians who voted for Trump, those who voted against him, and those who chose not to vote or voted third party. So if you perceive this book as having some kind of political agenda—to either condemn one side or endorse another—please understand that this is not my intention. My goal is to encourage us to think beyond the narrow confines of "cable politics." If we fail to do this, we risk losing the next generation.

2. THE DOUBTING

Still somewhat loyal to American Evangelicalism, the Doubting may have some serious questions about the Bible and Christianity. They may occasionally use the term *deconstructing,* but not often. That's because they might be tugging at the threads of American Evangelicalism, but they're still receptive to the Loyal's answers to their questions. They feel culturally at home in the movement. They don't feel so much discomfort in the church that they're ready to take a hike, but depending on how their questions are treated, this is a fork in the road. Some of them will pull back into the Loyal crowd. Others will continue to unthread American Evangelicalism and end up in the third category—the Disillusioned. For my readers who count themselves among the Doubting (and this may sound surprising), I don't want this book to bring you back into the Loyal crowd. If I do my job well, I'm hoping to bring you through a growth process beyond these categories.

3. THE DISILLUSIONED

The Disillusioned are—according to my own experience and Davis and Graham's research—a huge swath of the dechurched and those who use the term *deconstructing.* The Disillusioned still hold to orthodox Christian beliefs but feel disenfranchised not by evangelical convictions but by American evangelical subculture. They aren't questioning orthodoxy. They aren't even questioning the classic "Bebbington quadrilateral"[5] of evangelical beliefs: (1) the authority of Scripture, (2) the atonement of Jesus, (3) the need for rebirth by the Holy Spirit, and (4) a commitment to social and spiritual activism. These doctrinal commitments aren't the issue for these folks. Rather, they're questioning something Australian evangelical historian John Dickson calls the "Bully Church" syndrome particular to American evangelicals. Dickson noted that many evangelicals around the globe have stopped using the term *evangelical,* thanks to us:

> Evangelicals in Britain and Europe and Australia are very different from evangelicals here [in America]. And I've noticed, in the last ten years, lots of Australians who used to be happy going by *evangelical,* because they meant British evangelical—that gentle Anglicanism of William Wilberforce, socially engaged, happy to be in public, keen to see people evangelized with the Bible—they don't want to go by *evangelical* anymore.[6]

In other words, global evangelicals agree. American evangelicals need a vibe check. Our ethos is cynical. We're insecure about the future. Afraid. Apocalyptic in our outlook. Angry. Evangelical religion scholar John Stackhouse noted that "in America . . . evangelicals can think that they either run the country or they should. Nowhere else do evangelicals think that."[7] In other words, the difference between American evangelicals and global evangelicals is this: We're the *entitled.* That toxic American Evangelicalism is what so many millions of dechurched Americans are deconstructing. They will often use the word *deconstructing*—though I give it a more technical definition below—but what they're describing is disillusionment. They may have read Kristin Kobes Du Mez's *Jesus and John Wayne* or Jemar Tisby's *The Color of Compromise* or Tim Alberta's *The Kingdom, the Power, and the Glory.* They may have read Russell Moore's *Losing Our Religion* or Beth Moore's X (formerly Twitter) account and memoir *All*

My Knotted Up Life or listened to Mike Cosper's *The Rise and Fall of Mars Hill* podcast and felt a sense of haunting familiarity. It's not that the Disillusioned are ready to jump ship on faith, but they sense—rightly—that something is rotten in American evangelical Denmark, and they're not sure where else to turn.

If you find yourself among the Disillusioned with American Evangelicalism, I wrote this book for you. We don't need another book merely telling us to burn down the American evangelical project. We need a way forward toward renewal and restoration. That's what I hope to point you toward.

4. THE DECONSTRUCTING

The Deconstructing have experienced both doubts and disillusionment because of Bully Evangelicalism but taken it a bit further. The Deconstructing—where I once was—may consider themselves post-Bible or post-church Christians, looking for spirituality without all the American evangelical baggage. Often, these folks have a sense not only that American Evangelicalism isn't for them but also that it's deeply wrong and dangerous, perhaps because they themselves have experienced or witnessed the kinds of abuse—spiritual, emotional, physical—that Bully Evangelicalism culture makes so much space for. Folks in this crowd could properly be called "Deconstructing" in the sense that Yale literature professor Paul de Man (the great popularizer of the word) used it: the dismantling of previously accepted ideas because of the belief that they have no inherent meaning. Now, if you'd asked me what I was doing when I left the Bible and the church behind twenty years ago, I definitely would *not* have whipped out Paul de Man and claimed that Christianity had no inherent meaning. What I would have said, as a "post-Bible," "post-church" Christian, is that I had a high value for Jesus's words.

However, I had very little patience for the rest of the Bible. I had hardly any interest in what the global, historic church said about the Bible. If you brought up something in Scripture that crossed my sensibilities, I would have told you there are lots of different interpretations of the Bible, and I chose not to accept yours. I probably, however, never would have said "the Bible is wrong." Had I been deconstructing today, I may have described myself as redecorating a room or reassembling a boat or a house or something.

But years later, with help from wise friends, mentors, and the historic church, I can see in my past Deconstructing self twenty years ago an assumption deeply ingrained in me, and nearly every deconstructer I know: I assumed *I* was the architect of Christian faith. Me. *I* decided which interpretations to choose from. *I* decided which verses to emphasize. Deeply buried in this is the assumption that Christianity had no inherent meaning, but I would never have said it that way. This is why, throughout this book, I'm not going to talk about "reconstructing" faith. More on that later.

For now, I'll say this: The curious thing about the explosion of the term *deconstruction* in American Exvangelical culture today is that scholars have almost entirely stopped using the word. Why? Because in the academic world, this word fairly fell out of favor when—surprise!—it was discovered that Paul de Man's deconstruction philosophy was really a way to justify his insipid lifestyle. De Man, after his death, was exposed as "a bigamist, a convicted criminal, and a Nazi sympathizer."[8] The idea that all of life and language was meaningless, as it turned out, was a convenient way to excuse his choices. It makes sense, doesn't it? When someone— anyone—makes themselves and their own preferences, values, and desires the arbiter of truth, something is going to go awry, no matter what religion or ideology they claim.

So is there something to the critique, often made of proper

deconstructers, that behind their objections there lurks a simple unwillingness to follow Jesus into the hard things? To make Christian faith all about them? Maybe. Sometimes. Often. But here's the problem with lobbing grenades at this crowd: If you had said to me twenty years ago, "You're just Deconstructing because you love sin more than Jesus," I would have said, "You're just *Loyal* because you love sin more than Jesus!" The reason I was deconstructing in the first place was because, thanks to the culture of Bully Evangelicalism, the Christians around me interpreted the Bible in a way that let *them* continue in their biases, power-seeking habits, greed, and hatred.

But here's the key: *I was still searching.*

I was deconstruc*ting*, but I wasn't *departed.* I needed someone who both affirmed my critiques of Bully Evangelicalism and offered me an ancient, stirring vision of Jesus's love, beauty, and freedom that spoke to my deepest dreams. That's no simple task. This is why the process of healing for the Deconstructing is going to be much longer than it is for the Doubting or even the Disillusioned. For me, healing came slowly, in safe and thoughtful communities. My friend Ian Harber, author of the book *Walking Through Deconstruction,* once asked how long it took me to find healing after deconstructing my faith.

"About twelve years," I said. There was a long silence on the phone.

"That tracks," he said finally.

"How about for you?" I asked.

"About ten years." This range, for the Deconstructing, is generally true. I think the fastest process I've seen a true deconstructer go through, to feel renewed in their faith, is seven years. But that's because my friend Joseph—you'll read about his story in a later chapter—is such an intense personality and truth seeker that, honestly, walking through deconstruction and renewal for him was like doing it on steroids. I'd also like to think it was, in part, because he and I met regularly throughout the process, and after having fumbled my way through working with deconstructers for about a decade, I finally had a somewhat clear idea of what Joseph needed.

Sadly, rather than restoring the Deconstructing in a spirit of gentleness, our evangelical response tends to push them further away, catapulting the Doubting and Deconstructing into the Departed phase. So, yes, some evangelical critiques of deconstruction ring partially true: The fully Deconstruct*ed* might very well love sin more than Jesus. But at the end of the day, without loving and patient intervention, *we all do,* don't we? We should rightly condemn modern heretics, of course. But who is doing the work we're called to do in response to the wavering: "If anyone is caught in any transgression, you who are spiritual should restore him in a spirit of gentleness. Keep watch on yourself, lest you too be tempted. Bear one another's burdens, and so fulfill the law of Christ" (Galatians 6:1–2, ESV)? Or, more simply, which of us are seeking to obey this admonition from Jude: "Be merciful to those who doubt" (verse 22)? I also wrote this book for the Deconstructing, because it's the book *I* needed fifteen years ago.

5. THE DEPARTED

The Deconstruct*ing* are not the same as the *Departed.* The Departed may use the term "deconstruct*ed,*" but likely won't use the term "deconstruct*ing,*" because they have closed the door on faith altogether. Sometimes this is done with a public, cocksure, and optimistic posture. Oftentimes, however, I find that people who have departed did not feel they had control over the process. They are often left confused and saddened. They weren't sure why they lost their faith, but they did.

Here is something to keep in mind with this group: It is

incredibly hard to keep your faith in a secular world. And by incredibly hard, I mean impossible, at least from a natural viewpoint. We live in what Catholic philosopher Charles Taylor calls a "disenchanted" world—a world where Christianity is assumed not to matter to the way we go about our lives. That sort of thinking can really get to a guy, you know? Add to that all the online voices giving credible sounding arguments against the Christian faith, and I find it miraculous that any of us Westerners have faith at all. Deconstructing folks are often listening to these publicly departed folks and have lots of questions: Why does God allow evil? Why do some of the Old Testament commands seem sexist or racist or violent? Can we really trust the form of the Scriptures in the way we've received them? All very important questions that people have been thinking about and answering for centuries.

But this is *not* an apologetics book, trying to dismantle the arguments of publicly departed folks like Abraham Piper, Rhett and Link, or Joshua Harris. Here's why: Deconstructing and departed people tend to have a lot of intellectual hang-ups. But often, debates over these intellectual questions run in circles. That's because the reason why many people latch on to these arguments *in the first place* is because they've become disillusioned with the Christian faith (or at least the version we've presented them). They no longer *want* to believe it or feel motivated to fight for it. Until we can re-enchant people with an ancient, global, hope-filled vision of faith, all of our good and important intellectual arguments will be an exercise in treading water.

Merely answering intellectual objections to faith with a deconstructor is like analyzing the merits of the *Mona Lisa* by scanning it with a microscope. There's nothing wrong with this, of course. We could have all kinds of interesting conversations about the *Mona Lisa*'s origins, paint blends, materials, and so on. But none of those conversations would capture the *Mona Lisa*'s enigmatic smile, her all-seeing gaze, and the curious sense of longing she evokes. It would be pretty ridiculous to hear two people debate the merits of the *Mona Lisa* and whether it is a masterpiece by looking at it only through a microscope. In fact, until we've seen the beautiful portrait as a whole, why would we be motivated to dig into those little details at all? This book, then, is less about scanning around Christianity to talk about its controversial bits. The first thing we need to do is zoom out and see its big, sweeping picture of Jesus's dreams for humanity.

Only then do we have a context for these other important conversations.

MOVING FORWARD

Let me close with something surprising: I don't believe the Great Dechurching movement is all bad news—or even bad news at all. In fact, one of the reasons I love Redeemer Presbyterian in Indianapolis, where I'm an assistant pastor, is that Redeemer has a unique track record of helping the Deconstructing and Disillusioned find real healing and help. You may have read a bit about our work in *Walking Through Deconstruction*. If you visit our church, you're not going to find a typical evangelical atmosphere. We exist in the heart of a vibrant city, and our church is filled with weird art, songs you've never heard before, and quirky people of all ages. But it's also a haven for many who've felt left behind by Bully Evangelicalism. I'd guess at least half our congregation are folks who are disillusioned with American evangelical subculture and have probably been through some kind of deconstruction process. But they still maintain the convictions of "born again" Evangelicalism of the nineteenth century, committed to Jesus's atonement, the Scriptures' authority, and social activism.

Why are people disillusioned with American Evangelicalism attending—and finding renewal—at Redeemer? First and foremost, it's because of God's Spirit. But it's also because our church has a couple of characteristics they simply don't find elsewhere.

1. We're (way) out of step with American evangelical subculture.
2. We're hopeful about the future of the global, historic, evangelical church.

In other words, we allow people to experience their disillusionment and deconstruction, and in some measure, nearly all of us on staff share that. But we also urge people forward with a clear vision of participation in the global, historic church, as well as a hopeful and (I hope) compelling vision for following Jesus in our city. Rather than seeing people move from disillusionment into deconstruction, we've seen a new process take place:

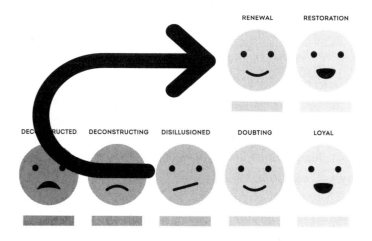

This is, of course, not possible for everyone's story. Apostasy is real, and sometimes it can't be stopped no matter how gracious, winsome, or truthful we are. I've certainly wept and prayed over people who've abandoned their families or slunk into a drug-induced despair or publicly disavowed their faith on social media to a swell of shallow affirmation. But certainly there is a measure of wisdom that I've also seen gently invite folks beyond American Evangelicalism into the global, historic church where they can experience not "reconstruction"—since this bears all the same individualistic assumptions of deconstruction (we'll talk more about this later)—but renewal and restoration.

This book mirrors the process that I've experienced and that I've had the privilege to walk deconstructing Christians through. Part 1, "Deconstruction," focuses on cynical dreams of Bully evangelicals. Part 2, "Restoration," connects us back to an ancient, global, hope-filled vision of Christian faith. Part 3, "Jesus's Dreams," points to nine ancient, historic—but often neglected—practices for finding renewal and restoration. In this last section, I'll tell you stories of how I've seen these practices change the lives of the Loyal, Doubting, Disillusioned, and Deconstructing people I know and love . . . including my own life. So, if you identify with one of the categories above, this book is absolutely written for you. But it's also designed as a book to work through *alongside* those in the categories above . . . a tool I desperately wish I'd had over the past fifteen years of ministry, in the hundreds of conversations I've had—both on a college campus and in the local church—with students and church members who identify as Deconstructing.

There's a children's book I read to my youngest son every night about a family going on a bear hunt. This nutty family—who must have the Mercedes-Benz of life insurance plans—

keeps going through rivers and forests and fields to find a grizzly bear. Bizarre, right? I do think they have some sound advice, though, because when they get stuck, they sing:

We can't go over it,
We can't go under it,
We've got to go through it![9]

Many conservatives have tried to go over the dechurching movement by taking back control of the White House, trying to enforce policies that give them a sense of nostalgia and security, and devoting hours to "studying" the issues by reading books and articles written by people who just so happen to look, think, and sound exactly like them. But this approach is actually accelerating secularism, not staving it off, as we'll see in the following chapter. On the other hand, many liberals have tried to go under the dechurching movement by adjusting their views on orthodoxy and ethics to accommodate the social moment. As Davis and Graham noted, however, the mainline church in America is declining even more rapidly than the evangelical movement.[10]

We can't go over deconstruction through coercion and power. We can't go under it by catering to the cultural headwinds. We've got to go through it.

I've seen many people dechurch over the past several years; it's true. It's heartbreaking. But in that same time, I've also seen far more people come to Jesus than I've seen before. I truly believe that if we meet the moment right, this isn't the end of something. It's the beginning. My prayer is that all of us—the Loyal, the Doubting, the Disillusioned, the Deconstructing . . . and, yes, even the Departed—can move away from the cynical dreams of Bully Evangelicalism *and* progressive Christianity to embrace the dreams of Jesus. And I have great hope that we will. As John Dickson wrote about the current fracturing of the American church,

> I dare to think it's more likely to be a positive moment than a negative moment. Because I think of American evangelicalism as a giant that's fallen asleep in a bit of a fog. And if American evangelicals can pivot in this moment and work out the answers to those questions—What does it mean to lose well? What does it mean to be cheerfully confident without being brash and arrogant and manipulative and controlling?—I think it will bless America, and I think it will bless the world.[11]

Like Dickson, I'm critical of American evangelical subculture. But I'm also deeply hopeful. I wrote this book because it's the book I needed as a Loyal evangelical. It's also the book I needed as a Doubting, Disillusioned, and Deconstructing Christian. I didn't need condemnation. I needed hope. So whether you're Loyal, Doubting, Disillusioned, or Deconstructing, this book is for you. I don't want to yank you back into the Loyal category. I also don't want to send you into the self-destructive spiral of the Departed. Rather, to quote The Doors' lead singer Jim Morrison, I want you to "break on through to the other side."[12] I want you to see how the global, ancient vision of Christianity isn't about fear and cynicism. It's about experiencing, embodying, and extending the light of Jesus. Jesus's story is about restoring love, beauty, and freedom to the world. It's a story that frees us to dream again.

Jesus wants *you* to be restored.

Re-storied.

PART 1

DECONSTRUCTION

2

Deconstructing

I would like to believe in God. I simply can't.
— TA-NEHISI COATES, *We Were Eight Years in Power*

The opposite of joy isn't sorrow—it's hopelessness.
— TIM KELLER, Twitter post

Annuit coeptis. I saw the phrase for the first time on January 6, 2021. I don't speak Latin, and I didn't understand what it meant, but it stuck. I was scrolling through my Twitter feed, watching as thousands of angry Americans barged into the nation's Capitol building. Chilling photos and footage appeared on my screen: a smiling man stealing a podium; Confederate flags fluttering in the halls; people dressed like barbarians, whooping and beating their chests. It looked like one of those 1950s alien invasion movies, except instead of aliens, it was people who looked like *me* . . . That was the most disturbing thing. It was all so familiar. The protesters' picket signs were scrawled with slogans I recognized:

"Jesus Is King!"
"Jesus Saves!"
"God, Guns & Guts Made America."[1]

Chris Tomlin's stadium pop ballad "How Great Is Our God"—a song I'd heard a million times growing up, in my mom's passenger van on the way to karate lessons—blared in the background. So as much as I desperately wanted to distance myself from those angry people, I couldn't. I knew, deep down, these were *my* crazy people.

That's because I grew up as an evangelical.

"This is *us*," I told myself. "This is *me. Don't look away.*"

In the following weeks, I heard virtually every evangelical leader feverishly "disavow" the events of the insurrection. But to me, these leaders' comments felt so hollow. It was like someone who lives off fried food trying to disavow their own heart attack. I'm no doctor, but I don't think you can really do that. I've been inside this evangelical mess long enough to know that we made it. We fed this tiger, and now that it's grown, we don't have any right to "disavow" it. The insurrection wasn't any kind of accident to the evangelical church.

It's what our dreams made.

During the weeks following the insurrection, I wondered what Jesus would be doing if He lived in America in 2021. I thought of another mob, filled with religious zeal and surrounding Jesus a week before His crucifixion. Jesus had entered Jerusalem riding on the back of a donkey, a sign of peace and humility.

"Blessed is the king who comes in the name of the Lord!" the crowds shouted. "Peace in heaven and glory in the highest!" (Luke 19:38). The gospel writer Luke said, at that moment, Jesus looked at the city . . . and wept (verse 41). Why? I suspect it's because Jesus knew the dagger of religious zeal is fickle. Days later, the same mouths proclaiming "Jesus is King!" would clamor for His death: "Crucify him!" (Matthew 27:22).

Jesus wasn't the kind of king people wanted—like the king of Rome or Persia or Greece. These people had big armies and beautiful palaces and expensive gel in their hair. Jesus wasn't like them. Caesar Augustus's name means "the Glorious One."[2] Jesus's name Immanuel means "God with us." Rome's "gospel of peace"—the Pax Romana—meant the conquest of others. But Jesus's gospel was about a gentle, humble, and suffering king coming to His people with meekness and vulnerability. People don't go for that kind of thing, because we don't want to *be* humble, suffering, or meek. We especially don't want to be vulnerable. We want a king who will protect us from those things.

The same was true of the religious leaders. They were happy to have a Messiah who would make Jerusalem great again. When Jesus told them that their dreams were sick and cynical and that He dreamed of true love, beauty, and freedom coming through His kingdom . . . they handily executed Him. We conservative religious people should never forget that the loudest voices calling for Jesus's crucifixion were religious people. The political leaders of Rome were just pawns. Good people—Scripture-believing, praying, family-focused people with conservative values—crucified Jesus, and they did it in God's name.

Whatever happened to Jesus's dreams? I wondered, weeks after I watched the mobs infiltrate the Capitol. Maybe the evangelical church wasn't such a unique little snowflake. Maybe the angry mobs calling for Jesus's crucifixion weren't so different from our own.

Maybe *I* would have crucified Jesus.

In the weeks following the insurrection, this question kept bubbling up: "Whatever happened to Jesus's dreams?" And every time, a nagging voice kept whispering, "We've crucified them."

I looked up that phrase *annuit coeptis.* It's been inscribed on the American Capitol's walls since its construction. It means "God has favored our undertakings."

CYNICAL DREAMS

It was 4:45 A.M., weeks after the insurrection.

The previous four years, I'd worked with college students at the University of Missouri, so I was out late a lot, typically eating my feelings with a cup of Oreo Speedwagon from Sparky's Homemade Ice Cream. This was a real problem, since in middle age, my body started shaking me awake at 4:45 most mornings.

Charles Dickens had the same problem, I remembered, lying awake one particular morning. He solved it, I once heard, by taking walks through the early-morning streets of London. I kept lying in bed, thinking how romantic it sounded to be Charles Dickens, strolling through the city, saying hello to stray dogs. But then I got to wondering whether he knew about Jack the Ripper, and I decided he probably didn't, so instead of going for a walk, I turned on the television.

I cringed as I flipped through all my accumulated apps and streaming services. *I should cancel those,* I thought, but something caught my eye. With two hours to spare before my family woke up and six hours before my college students, I had just enough time for a 1990s romantic comedy starring Kevin Costner. Now I don't want to give the impression I'm crazy about rom-coms. I feel the same way about them as I do about someone else's dog peeing on my lawn—if it's happening, it's not like I *won't* watch. The real selling point of the movie was the front cover, with a picture of Kevin Costner on a pitcher's mound, holding a baseball and looking like a real man's man, which I now think was a trick to get men to watch this rom-com with their girlfriends.

It wasn't really about baseball, like *at all.*

Whatever happened to romantic comedies? I thought. *They were so light, so predictable, so cheesy. So great!* The film began just like I suspected it would. A handsome, rogue millionaire is living like a desperado, directionless, searching for love. Kelly Preston's car breaks down, and there he is. *Bam!* They make small talk, then they go on a romantic New York City date. How they ended up in New York City, I had no idea. The film hit some real low points in the middle and didn't seem to be going anywhere, especially the part where the couple was in Kevin Costner's kitchen, discussing whether they liked dark- or light-meat chicken. But things turned around, and the film wrapped up just like I hoped it would, with the couple finding each other in the airport and having a big, sloppy make-out session. Great! Cut to credits, cue the sappy country song.

It was 7:00 A.M. by then. I poured coffee, thinking about the film and the story it told—a story about a *dream*, the universal dream of romance. I thought again about the question of where rom-coms had gone. They didn't make movie-theater headlines anymore. Come to think of it, people don't even make movie theaters anymore. The truth was, my college students wouldn't watch even half of a film like that. They were pretty jaded about airports and making out. Well, they weren't jaded about making out. But they didn't believe in Romance with a capital *R*, the dream the film was selling. They didn't watch many films with happy endings. To borrow some terms from Netflix, they watched "gritty" films with "dark themes." It took me about two years of working with students to understand that if there is one word to describe this generation—and our culture at large—it's *cynical.*

Two months ago, during a sermon to my college students, I asked whether I was right about that. "Are you guys cynical?" I asked. "It seems like you don't really have much hope for the future." Big nods all around. They wanted to talk about it.

"Where does all the cynicism come from?" I asked them.

One very bright student raised his hand. "I thought you could tell us," he said.

The room laughed, but I didn't. It made me sad.

Before my time in college ministry, I worked with high school students for a decade. Every year, I did a bit about the Disney film *Tangled,* a retelling of the story of Rapunzel. In the Disney version, Rapunzel is rescued by a handsome rogue named Flynn Rider, who is a thief. I told the students Disney needed to write a sequel. It would be the story of how Flynn became bored with royalty and eventually abandoned Rapunzel for some other Valley girl in a tower, ending his days eating Doritos while grifting cash from the royal treasury as a side hustle.

"So, kids," I'd say, "the moral is that even if a dashing man *does* offer to rescue you from a tower, you should still *never* marry a kleptomaniac. The end."

Ten years ago, my high school students trashed me for that bit. I was trying to convince them the dream Disney was selling—the dream of romance and of a big, strong, clever man who would fix all their problems—was fake. They didn't believe me.

Today, it's different.

I tried telling this story to my college students. They were not shocked. They were bored. They looked at me as if to say, "Yeah, so? What else is new?" They made me feel like I'd kicked a bunch of those troll dolls right in their cute little chins. How quickly the world had changed. The students I worked with on campus weren't dreamers. They were survivalists, paralyzed with anxiety about gun violence, sexual assault, global warming, hypocritical churches, racial disparities, and political fights. The best they could do? Duck and cover. The news shows campuses filled with radical, angry protestors. I wish. Mostly they're just filled with disillusioned, depressed young people checked out in their dorm rooms, eating Flamin' Hot Cheetos and streaming videos of people experimenting with elephant toothpaste. And I believe there is a reason my students act this way: This is the world *we've* handed them. Society, yes. But the church also.

The church—just like the world—is filled with cynical dreams.

WHY I'M TERRIBLE AT FUNDRAISING

I raise money for my job, so I often travel around the country and speak to Sunday schools. I've learned to expect certain questions from parents and church members.

"Do you think young people are starting to believe in evolution instead of the Bible?"

"No, I don't think so," I say. "They mostly believe in both." I assure them I do not believe humans evolved from monkeys, but having grown up with four brothers, I can see why some would think that.

"Are the liberals on your campus keeping you from doing your job?"

"No, they are pretty friendly to me."

"Are college students falling for the cultural Marxism of their professors?"

"I don't know what those words mean. I mostly talk to them about Jesus, and to be honest, we don't really cover economics."

The concern of the older members is genuine. They can see the next generation slipping through their fingers. I often smile and suppress what I would say if I weren't asking them for money to do my job. But there is a new question I've heard recently, and it's given me permission to say just a little more:

"What do you do with students who are deconstructing their faith?"

I take a deep breath. "I help them." Blank stares.

"You mean you help them *re*construct their faith?" they ask.

"No," I say. "I mean I help them *deconstruct* their faith."

They shift in their seats. If I'm in this deep, I might as well keep digging, right?

"We are losing the next generation; it's true," I say. "I watch it happen in real time. But almost every exvangelical student says the same thing to me: They aren't deconstructing because of their liberal professors; they are deconstructing *because of the church.* So, I help them. I help them see that much of what we call Christianity in evangelical circles is more about a cultural project than it is about Jesus. When they say the church is too political, hypocritical, and racist, I tell them I agree. I need to do that for about a year before they start listening to me. I share with students how important it was for me to deconstruct my own evangelical upbringing before I could take faith seriously."

Wallets close.

Hey, I never said I was *good* at raising money.

I gave that terrible stump speech years ago based on intuition and experience. Recently, however, some smart statisticians have shown this is, most definitely, the case. The dechurched aren't leaving because they reject Christian orthodoxy. They're leaving because they reject evangelical *culture.*[3] Among dechurched evangelicals, about two-thirds expressed that their parents' evangelical faith played a role in pushing them away from church. Why? The top five responses follow:

1. All their emphasis on culture war lost me over time (14%)

2. Their lack of love, joy, gentleness, kindness, and
   generosity (14%)
3. Their inability to listen (14%)
4. Their inability to engage with other viewpoints
   (13%)
5. Their racial attitudes or actions (13%)[4]

Yeah, that tracks. Over the years, I've had hundreds of
these conversations with students. I've learned to shift my
goals. I no longer work to help them "reconstruct" their faith.
For one, that feels like too much work. And for two, reconstruction isn't what students need. What they need is *renewal.*
They need *restoration.* To be *re-storied.* My students and we
evangelicals need a new story. A better story. A story that
ends not in cynicism but in hope. And that, I believe, is what
the true gospel, the original gospel of Jesus, gives to the
world. Hope. Tangible, real, feel-it-in-your-gut hope. Just the
other day, I read an article by a Gen Z writer named Luke
Simon, speaking to the endless doomscrolling culture we live
in. He said something profound: "I craved my phone not for
its screen, or for its addictive entertainment, or even as an
escape. What I truly craved was *hope.*"[5] Will Luke Simon find
what he's looking for in the American evangelical church?
Will he find *hope*? Or will we give him one more reason to
doomscroll his life away?

I keep having these conversations with students because I
believe there is a Christian faith older than our American
dreams. Before *annuit coeptis,* there was *lema sabachthani*
("My God, my God, why have you forsaken me?"). Jesus's
kingdom-sized dreams of love, beauty, and freedom, crucified on the cross, are a far cry from "God has favored our
undertakings," aren't they? And yet it's the very subversive-
ness of Jesus's dreams, their *rejectedness,* that makes them so
miraculous. Jesus's dreams, so much less likely than ours, are

in the end realized through His resurrection. He's the only Dreamer whose dreams come true. He's the only Dreamer we can trust. Jesus is the only man standing absolutely on the right side of history. And that should give us hope.

HOPE OVER CEREAL

"Would they see hope in your eyes?"

I was standing before four hundred members of an evangelical church. I told them all the things I just told you: the cynicism in my students, the anxiety, the pain, and the depression.

"We live in a country filled with despair. It's growing with every hour. I can see it in the eyes of the next generation. If I brought them to your church, would they find what they're looking for? Would they find *hope*? Would they see light in your eyes?" I told them my students were only a sample size of a growing trend. I told them about a study by David Brooks published in *The Atlantic,* which says, compared to a decade ago, Americans are less likely to trust the government (only 10 percent of Gen Zers "trust politicians to do the right thing"). They are less likely to think other people are trustworthy (40 percent to 19 percent). Millennials believe "most of the time, people look out for themselves" (73 percent) and that others "would try to take advantage of you if they got a chance" (71 percent). Brooks called this a culture of "explosive distrust" and said if we don't fix it, society will go down the toilet hole.[6] My words, not his.

I reminded the church about the hope of Jesus.

"We've buried Jesus's dreams in a drawer. Where are they?"

After the talk, people thanked me and told me I was brave to tell the truth. I didn't feel brave. I felt like I was in one of those dreams where your legs move as if they're churning through a tub of overheated bubble gum. I reminded this church they have the answer to my students' cynicism: hope. And by hope, I didn't mean some wishy-washy thing like "I hope there are some Oreos left in the pantry, but I'm pretty sure I ate the last two sleeves last night." Hope, in the Bible, isn't a wish. It's an expectation. Paul said the three great virtues of the Christian life are "faith, hope and love" (1 Corinthians 13:13). Do we really suppose that Paul was saying a mature Christian is all about "faith, wishful thinking, and love"? I don't think so. Hope is a clear, anchored vision of the kingdom future, given to us by Jesus Himself. It's not a wish; it's a promise to us. But it feels like nobody in the evangelical church has that. Even as I was speaking, I pictured everyone going back to their homes and devoting more hours to cable news and social media than the message of the Bible. I could already see the scales of cynicism building over their eyes as I spoke. I know the one thing the world needs—*hope*—is the one thing outsiders aren't likely to find in the evangelical church.

"Always be prepared to give an answer," wrote the apostle Peter, "to everyone who asks you to give the reason for *the hope* that you have" (1 Peter 3:15). When I've heard preachers talk about this verse, they've said, "Peter tells us we need to be ready to defend our faith. We need to give evidence for what we believe." I always squirmed when I heard that. Was Peter really telling low-income Middle Easterners to give philosophical proofs for God's existence to their neighbors? Not that that kind of thing is wrong. It just never seemed very likely to me. Peter seemed to be talking about something deeper: *hope.* I did raise my hand one time to ask a pastor about this.

"Um, I thought the reason for our hope was Jesus," I said. "Isn't Peter just telling people to be filled with hope? And then to tell people about Jesus?" The pastor looked at me like

I was from Mars. Talking about hope in my evangelical setting was like that. When was the last time you heard someone
ask an evangelical, "Could you please tell me about the wonderful hope you have in humanity's future?" I've never heard
that. I hope you have, in your circles, but I never have.

Jesus says the church has something to offer to this world:
a dream. If we lose that dream, we've lost everything. "The
eye is the lamp of the body," Jesus said. "If your eyes are
healthy, your whole body will be full of light. But if your eyes
are unhealthy, your whole body will be full of darkness"
(Matthew 6:22–23). In the ancient world, the eyes were the
symbol of desire. The thing before your eyes is the thing for
which you yearn and hope. Jesus is speaking to the power of
our dreams—dream badly, and you will become a ghost;
your eyes will grow dim. Dream well, and your eyes will light
up like a kid on Christmas Day. People will want to be a part
of that thing you see. Cambridge psychologist Brian Little
once said that, to a psychologist, the most important thing
about us isn't what type of person we are—our Enneagram
number, Myers-Briggs letters, or Hogwarts school. Rather,
it's our dreams that are most core to who we are, or what
Little calls "personal projects." Find a generally agreeable
Ravenclaw whose child isn't getting proper attention at the
hospital, and she'll become a Slytherin before you can say
"Mischief managed."[7] Personality tells us *what you are like.*
Dreams tell us *who you are.*

So, church, how are we dreaming these days?

Is there light in our eyes?

The other morning, my son looked me straight in the eye
and said, "So, Dad, what's your true potential?"

My true potential? "Little Nordic Viking kids would never
have asked that question," I said. "Now go eat your cereal."

He looked confused.

"Okay, why?" I asked. "What's *your* true potential?"

"Not sure yet," he said, happily chomping away at his sugar bombs. To be honest, I think he got the phrase *true potential* from a Lego show. But his question was genuine. He was searching for something in my eyes: hope.

What did he see in my eyes? I wondered.

Did he see light?

Did he see cynicism?

Or hope?

3

Exclusion

Sure, burn it down, easy. Annihilating is easy. Razing things to the ground is easy. Trying to fix what's broken is hard. Hope is hard.

—LOKI

His eyes were dead; the light had gone out.

—VICTOR HUGO, *Les Misérables*

The year I arrived on the University of Missouri's campus was also the inaugural year of Donald Trump's presidency. One night, in the heat of election season, I broached the topic to one of my college students after Bible study. "So, what do you think about all this?" I said. I expected him to go off on a rant, because that's what the kids on social media do. But all he did was shrug.

"What, political stuff?" he said. "My parents care about that. I think it's all a bunch of garbage."

"Really?" I said. "I thought you would be . . . I don't know . . . a little more *jazzed* about it."

"Nope," he said, excusing my inexcusable Dad slang. "Don't care. Everyone is just crazy these days."

As I met with students through my first semester, I heard the same thing. There were a few radical Left and Right students, sure. But most of them just felt like aliens in a foreign land. The most concerning thing to me was this: The students who felt out of place politically *also* felt out of place in the church.

"During the election season, my pastor kept talking about politics every Sunday," said one student from a more progressive church. "I felt like he should be teaching the Bible. So my family stopped going. I didn't think a pastor should be doing that." His progressive pastor—in trying to protect Christianity—had made this student feel like left-wing political policy *was* Christianity. If he didn't buy into the church's politics, maybe he wasn't a Christian after all.

A few weeks later, I met with a student named Rebecca, who grew up in a conservative church and attended a Christian school. The first time we met, she told me she was a feminist, but I already knew that because she had pink hair. Rebecca was cynical about all things Christian because her church, during her high school years, was scandalized by the pregnancy of one of her friends. That girl was "disciplined" by the church and promptly expelled. The boy who impregnated her? No consequences. That situation gave the election season some metaphorical weight for Rebecca. She watched these same church leaders wave aside Donald Trump's claims to sexually assault women as "locker-room talk." She heard them dismiss thousands of similar stories of women all over America. She watched her church critique the Black community's stories of injustice as forms of "neo-Marxism." Maybe, she thought, the church wasn't about Jesus at all. Maybe it was just about the stories of insecure White men.

"I'm done," she said. "I don't even recognize these people. If this is what the church is all about, I can't stand by it." She left the church, and I could only slow her way out the door.

Eventually these conversations started to feel like a recurring bad dream. It was a dream I had seemingly every afternoon—same stories, different students. Sometimes I was able to convince a student to hang on a little longer, to investigate Jesus and to try to separate their experience from the original Christian faith. I was lucky to have several students stick around, but even then, it took years to undo the church's damage, and I imagine their healing from church wounds will take a lifetime. What these students grew up with was a faith that offered personal safety at all costs, not sacrificial purpose. It was more interested in triumph over our enemies—or those who are just culturally different—than transformation. They were shown that Christianity was a small, cynical dream. There is a reason I care about their stories so much.

I was one of those kids.

THE CAMP WITH NO MARSHMALLOWS

My mother became a believer in Jesus when I was still wearing Batman underpants, and don't ask me when that phase ended. All you need to know is my mom was a real cool cat who grew up in the 1970s and did all the groovy hippie things groovy hippies did. Nobody taught my mom how to be a Christian, because no one in her family went to church. In fact, my mother was such a radical hippie that she met Jesus sitting on her bed, reading the gospel of John, tripping out on a vision of a cross of light beaming through her window. I mean tripping out metaphorically, of course, because I'm too afraid to ask her if it really is a metaphor.

Like I said, she was a real cool cat.

After that, she started going to church and watching movies about the end times and listening to Christian cassette tapes explaining how to help her future teenager stay a Christian through puberty. A few years after her conversion, she fell in with a weird niche group of other ex-hippies in the Detroit area who saw the whole Christian thing as one big, groovy experiment. They were all sending their kids to something called Worldview Camp in Tennessee, so she asked me if I wanted to go.

"Camping in Tennessee sounds good," I said. The camp was at Bryan College, right next to the old courtroom where William Jennings Bryan argued against teaching evolution in schools, which they told us was the grand showdown where Bryan stood up for America and Christianity. But as it turns out, he lost. I guess the location of the Worldview Camp was symbolic or something, about how one day we could overturn that ruling and make it illegal to teach evolution in schools, and then Christianity wouldn't be losing. We would be winning. We could make America great again.

Annuit coeptis.

After the Worldview Camp leaders explained all this, I asked a friend when all the camping was supposed to start. He explained that, here, the word *camp* meant lots of seminars, not actual camping or hiking or bonfires and maybe not even any s'mores. I can't say I was too disappointed, except about the s'mores, since I was the kid who snuck books into my hunting jacket when I was supposed to be becoming a man by sniping whitetails on crisp Michigan fall mornings. I actually took a shine to Worldview Camp after a couple of days because I was learning a lot, and I especially liked how, unlike real camping, there was always free juice in the cafeteria. Besides, during my seminars, I learned something I never realized: Jesus had one clear opinion on everything. I learned we could know Jesus's opinion on science and art and politics and literature and psychology and philosophy and history and dating, *especially* dating. But at Worldview Camp it wasn't called "dating." It was called "courting." Because castles are more Christian than anything you can think of, right? *Right?* Of course they are. You wouldn't question castles unless you were an absolute pagan.

The teachers at Worldview Camp quoted lots of philosophers, but my favorite part was when they quoted lyrics of the emo punk rock band Linkin Park, which they said represented a nihilistic worldview. But I thought those lyrics represented an honest worldview, so ironically they're the only words I remember from the seminars. The teachers explained how in college, liberal professors would try to sneak attack my Christian worldview, so I needed to be ready to defend Jesus's perspective on economics and literature and history and America. All of this made me feel a strange mixture of anxiety and bloodlust. But I did like how the world made sense to me after this experience. It felt good to know Jesus would have voted the same way everyone in my conservative church voted and He would have defended the Constitution and free markets and gun ownership. Maybe *I* would even be a speaker at Worldview Camp someday. Then I would mention how *I* once asked a humiliating question to *my* professor and how she was converted *that very afternoon.* I really wanted it to be *that very afternoon,* because I wasn't sure how else to end a story like that and also because I wanted to make sure people knew she was converted because of my worldview skills.

I did have a few questions about the whole thing, but I was sure it was only because of my deeply secularized worldview. *Thanks, liberals.* My questions started the last day of Worldview Camp. I was part of a team that would get up on stage and encourage everyone to go to a local shopping mall and try to convert people to our Christian worldview. I stood up on stage, and my friend said my voice went a few octaves higher—as if my anxiety put me in a kind of prepubescent trance—as I told everyone how urgent our trip to the shopping mall was. I was quite certain there was nothing psychologically significant about my reverting to boyhood when I talked about fighting for my mother's religion. But my friend's feedback did make me wonder whether, deep down, I really believed everything I was saying. So I decided to prove to myself—and everyone—that I did. Later that afternoon at the mall, I saw a muscular man with a shopping bag, sitting at the penny wishing fountain, waiting for his wife. I approached him, perhaps because my true worldview was masochism.

And he was converted that very afternoon. At least, that's how I hoped the story would end. Instead it went more like this:

"Pretty weird weather today, huh?" I said.

He glared at me.

"Uh, you come here a lot?"

Macho Man remained unresponsive, so I looked at his bag, trying to pick up on his interests and hobbies. "You like Victoria's . . . oh, I see."

Long silence this time. He was looking at me like a bug he was thinking of crushing. Finally, Macho Man spoke. "Now why would *I* want to talk to *you*?" he said.

My brain did a quick scan of all the worldview seminars, but nothing was registering.

I was sure, based on my worldview evangelism training, the next right question was "So anyway, if you died today, would you go to heaven and why?" That was the Big Question, after greasing the wheels by getting to know someone. Worldview Camp wasn't exactly a Dale Carnegie course. But in this moment, I started to wonder whether Macho Man would think it was weird that *I* was thinking about what *he* was thinking about *his own personal death* just a few seconds after meeting him. And because I tend to get very existential about things that don't at all need to be, his question really got to me. Why *would* he want to talk to me? What was I offering him? What did I have that he didn't? What did evangelicals have that he could possibly want? Why would our culture at large want anything to do with evangelical subculture? He put words to the questions I'd been asking myself all week. So I clenched my jaw and thought long and hard about the Big Question about death.

I looked Macho Man right in the eyes. And I cried. "I'm sorry," I said. He couldn't know it, but I really meant it. I stood up, and all the thick worldview books fell out of my bag and scattered uselessly at Macho Man's feet, which was yet another unnecessarily existential metaphor for my feelings in the moment.

I once heard a theologian named Dr. Soong-Chan Rah state that theological liberals are people who say cultures' opinions are more important than the Bible's opinions. That means, Dr. Rah said, evangelicals like to say they are conservative, but they are *actually* liberals. They are more interested in protecting *their* culture, comfort, and preferences than following God's dreams.

I'd say that's a pretty good summary of how I felt about Evangelicalism after Worldview Camp.

RAP

My first job in a church was on the south side of Indianapolis in a little trailer park village. I liked the village and the people in it, but truth be told, the church I worked at gave me the willies. My first day on the job, I walked into the sanctuary and saw a giant American flag on stage. I thought maybe it was a temporary placement, but it turns out the flag was part of the church's worship service, right alongside the pulpit and the choir. The pastor sat me down and said that I was to use

only the King James Bible and that I needed to be teachable.
I asked why the King James Version of the Bible was so important, since King James lived fifteen hundred years after
Jesus's disciples in continental Europe. He explained to me
that God works just like we expect Him to, and if He doesn't,
He can't be God. I told him it didn't make sense to *me* why
Jesus would have had twelve Jewish disciples in His lifetime
and then a thirteenth White one named King James fifteen
hundred years later so he could write the true Bible for us.
The pastor said all that didn't matter and told me to stop asking questions.

I learned a lot after that, and I tried to be teachable. I
learned that America was going to hell in a handbasket, and I
learned southern gospel songs, crooning about wanting to
leave this ol' world to go off to heaven far, far, far away. At
the end of every service, the pastor had everyone close their
eyes and raise their hands if they wanted to accept Jesus as
their Savior. He said, "I see that hand" many times each Sunday, which was impressive at first, but then it was confusing
because the same people were at church every week. The
math didn't exactly add up.

In the meantime, I was working with a youth group of
forty to fifty low-income students from the trailer park. I
asked the pastor if we could start a reading program for the
kids in the church or think about building a skate park so
they'd have something to do after school. The pastor said that
I was focusing too much on social things and that all I needed
to do was preach the Bible, get the kids saved, and go home.

"But here is another thing," I said. "They don't really *understand* the King James Bible."

"Well, they used to," he said.

"But they don't," I said.

"Well, they should!" he said.

"So what do you want me to do about that?" I asked. "Do

you want me to start a tutoring program so I can teach them how to read seventeenth-century English?"

I'm not saying I was being an angel. Also, I don't think the folks who went to the church were bad people, because at least one of them found a way to start a food pantry, even if it was against the church's theology about getting saved. But after a few months, it became clear my wife and I couldn't stay. Stories of abuse, perversion, and cover-up from the leadership came leaking out. We experienced this abuse in various ways (I won't go into them for our privacy), all of which have lingering effects on our lives today. The pastor gave himself and others a pass on these behaviors, however, because our church was based on God's "grace." I liked God's grace and all, but I was confused by the way the pastor used that word. To him it seemed to mean a lot of things, like how the pastor could be in charge of people's lives, hire sexual predators if he thought they'd help his ministry, and take financial advantage of young couples. Grace was flexible that way, and grace seemed to be working out pretty well for him, although it wasn't working out so well for the trailer park community.

I couldn't understand a faith that looked so little like Jesus's life on earth, all in the name of "grace." It was hard for me to picture a lot of hungry and sick people sitting around Jesus and Him saying, "We're not going to focus on your worldly needs, but anyway, who wants to be a follower of mine? *I see that hand.*" They would raise their hands, and Jesus would send them back to their normal lives, because now they could leave this ol' world someday and go far, far, far away to heaven.

Up until this point, I didn't think I cared about theology. But at this church I saw that bad theology can be a weapon. It can destroy people's lives. It can abuse people. It can justify all kinds of ugly things. The more I spent time in this church, the more it seemed like Worldview Camp: We were using *Jesus* to protect *us*.

One moment made this all clear to me.

A few months into my time at the church, I was hosting an after-school program and playing some Christian rap for the students. We were interrupted by pounding footsteps from the church offices upstairs. I ran up to see what was the matter, and I was met in the hallway by the pastor, who looked as red as if he'd just swallowed a whole chicken drumstick.

"What is this crap?" he said, gesturing to the radio.

"Oh," I said. "It's Christian rap music. Our students listen to rap, and I thought it would be good to introduce them to it."

"Listen," he said, pointing his finger at me. "If *I* can't understand it, it's not Christian! Turn it off!"

I've thought about that a lot over the years, and it's a pretty good summary of Bully Evangelicalism's theory about life. If we can't understand it, it's not Christian.

PHARISEES

The Pharisees were orthodox, Scripture-believing conservatives who tried to make the Scripture's teaching apply to daily life. They spent hours every day studying it in its original languages. They took mission trips to convert people. They spoke out against the evils of the Roman Empire and prayed for a day when the Messiah would bring them back into power. Their beliefs seemed to match most of Jesus's beliefs. They said they wanted to follow all of Scripture's commandments and teach people to do the same thing.

But Jesus said many of them had one major problem: They had no light in their eyes. "The eye is the lamp of the body. If your eyes are healthy, your whole body will be full of light. But if your eyes are unhealthy, your whole body will be full of darkness" (Matthew 6:22–23). Many Pharisees gave lip service to the Bible, but inside they had dark dreams. These are Jesus's public words about the Pharisees:

> Everything they do is done for people to see: They make their phylacteries wide and the tassels on their garments long; they love the place of honor at banquets and the most important seats in the synagogues; they love to be greeted with respect in the marketplaces and to be called "Rabbi" by others. . . .
>
> You shut the door of the kingdom of heaven in people's faces. You yourselves do not enter, nor will you let those enter who are trying to. . . .
>
> You travel over land and sea to win a single convert, and when you have succeeded, you make them twice as much a child of hell as you are. . . .
>
> Woe to you, teachers of the law and Pharisees, you hypocrites! You give a tenth of your spices—mint, dill and cumin. But you have neglected the more important matters of the law—*justice, mercy and faithfulness.* (Matthew 23:5–7, 13, 15, 23)

Pharisaism wasn't all bad. In fact, Jesus sometimes took the Pharisees' side in debates. For example, Jesus thought they were right about the resurrection and sometimes about moral issues, and at least He noticed the cute little tassels they were wearing. For instance, He seemed to agree with much of the Pharisees' moral teaching: "You must be careful to do everything they tell you." The problem was, the Pharisees didn't have the kind of hope-filled vision that transformed them to obey these things from the heart: "But do not do what they do, for they do not practice what they preach" (Matthew 23:3). The gospel writers don't present the Pharisees as irredeemable jerks. Nicodemus, who "must be born again" (John 3:7), was a famous and exemplary Pharisee convert. Paul himself was a Pharisee (Acts 23:6), and presumably thousands of Jewish leaders converted in the book of Acts were conservative Pharisees (2:41). So by repeating Jesus's critiques, I'm not trying to demonize this crowd.

Rather, I'm trying to follow Jesus's path and challenge the Pharisees among us (as a recovering Pharisee myself) to *dig deeper:* "You should have practiced the latter, without neglecting the former" (Matthew 23:23). They should have been practicing justice, mercy, and faithfulness *while also* being zealous about detailed scriptural issues. Jesus didn't say, "Stop being so obsessed with the Scriptures" or even, "Stop obeying those little details." He was saying, "You've missed the big picture. You've put the wrong emPHAsis on the wrong sylLAble. If you want to be part of My kingdom, you need to dream God's kingdom dreams, bringing My love, freedom, and beauty to every nation." The way the Pharisees taught the Bible excluded the poor, the stranger, and the marginalized. It also excluded people outside Jewish culture who were genuinely interested in the Jewish God Yahweh. When they found a convert, the Pharisees forced him into their own image and made him "twice as much a child of hell" as they were. And so their religion added up to this: "You shut the door of the kingdom of heaven in people's faces." That's not obeying the Bible. That's a form of cultural supremacy. As religious as they seemed, the Pharisees just didn't get it. They read and practiced the Scriptures as a cynical story of *exclusion.*

This has always been a temptation for people. "If I can't understand it, it's not Christian!" It's easy to forget I'm holding an ancient book from another time and cultural world. But reading the Bible with my own cultural lenses means I end up making Christianity in my own culture's image. Obedience becomes "Be like me!" This turns the Bible into a story of *exclusion*. It can happen in the White conservative church and in the progressive church too.

Progressive Christianity's exclusion is more subtle. It sounds nice, and to be honest, it's very attractive to me. The problem is, to fully buy into the progressive Christian way of life, we would need to *exclude* nearly every other culture, time, and place in church history. That includes our African American neighbors, who often hold to historic Christian teaching in areas where White liberal Christians squirm.

Esau McCaulley, African American theologian and *New York Times* columnist, made this point in his fantastic book *Reading While Black*. McCaulley talked about attending a progressive seminary and being told he had only two ways to interpret the Bible: White Conservatism or White Progressivism.

> When I walked into my first Bible class, I unknowingly entered the hundred years' war between white evangelicals and white mainline Protestants. My professors displayed sympathy for the latter. Their goal was to rid their students of the white fundamentalism that they believed was the cause of every ill that beset the South. A better South was the progressive South of the white mainline church. *It seems that in their minds, a progressive South was only possible when we rejected the centrality of the Bible for something more* fundamental, *namely the white mainline Protestant consensus on politics, economics, and religion.* . . .
>
> My professors had a point. One does not have to dig

very far into history to see that fundamentalist Christians in the South (and the North) have indeed inflicted untold harm on Black people. They have used the Bible as justification for their sins, personal and corporate. But there is a second testimony possibly more important than the first. That is the testimony of Black Christians who saw in *that same Bible* the basis for their dignity and hope in a culture that often denied them both. . . .

The question isn't always which account of Christianity uses the Bible. The question is which does justice to as much of the biblical witness as possible.[1]

Where is Jesus in the middle of all this? Jesus begins a project to bring together conservative Pharisees (Paul and Nicodemus), cultural elites (the Roman centurion and Matthew the tax collector), and, yes, even insurrectionists (Simon the Zealot) into His kingdom. Jesus continues this project in the book of Acts, where He commands His disciple Peter, "Do not call anything impure that God has made clean" (Acts 10:15). This was Jesus's way of saying that the gospel isn't about one culture. It's for everybody, even if you find their culture icky. Peter needed to repent of his cultural exclusion. At the same time, Jesus kept calling Gentiles away from their "live and let live" way of life. This call disturbed everybody, but especially the cultural elites, who complained, "They are all defying Caesar's decrees, saying that there is another king, one called Jesus!" (Acts 17:7). Under Jesus's rule, there is *no* room for cultural supremacy—not for the elites of Rome and not for the conservative Jews. Everyone's welcome to God's table, but no one should expect to sit comfortably. The dream of Jesus is bigger than the exclusion of both conservative White supremacy *and* progressive cultural elitism.

One of my favorite comedians, Jack Handey of *Saturday*

Night Live, once said, "Consider the rose. Now while you're doing that, I'll be over here digging through your wallet." It's almost too easy for Satan to keep the church distracted and convinced the enemy is somewhere "out there." The enemy is the Left. Or the enemy is the Right. And then we become so obsessed with that enemy that we can't see the dangers on our own sides. In ourselves. Over time, the "gospel" becomes a project of cultural exclusion, all in Jesus's name. Jesus's name becomes a weapon instead of a gift.

4

Relevance

I am not the reason no one trusts you
No one knows what you believe. . . .
You stand only for yourself, it's what you do.
—LIN-MANUEL MIRANDA, "Your Obedient Servant," *Hamilton*

There is no church I'm familiar with over the past 2000
years that I would be a member of if it were up to me. . . .
Yet I have little time for the anti-church crowd who seem
snobbish and who have little sense of the lived way of soul
and Christ.
—EUGENE PETERSON, quoted in *A Burning
in My Bones* by Winn Collier

A few years ago I met with a sophomore, Katy, who grew up in a church that preached inspirational messages. Every week she would walk away feeling inspired by what the preacher said—to pursue her dreams, overcome her bad habits, love herself, and have a more positive attitude.

"But I've been thinking about it," Katy said to me. "And I realized I could get all that advice from a podcast. And I was thinking, *Why would I go to church when I could hear that from a motivational speaker?*" I told her it was a good question. Maybe, I said, she should look for a church that taught something she *couldn't* hear anywhere else: the radical, revolutionary story and message of Jesus. Katy did end up doing just that, and now she's doing amazing work with healing trauma in Jesus's name. Life isn't easy, but she's found so much more satisfaction in following in Jesus's footsteps in a church community that puts Him at the center of life. But what she put into words about her church growing up isn't uncommon.

In an article called "The Sad Irony of Celebrity Pastors"—one that I think is both poignant and hilarious—Ben Sixsmith puts to words better than I can why the kind of church Katy described would never attract him. He's talking about a recent controversy with a NYC pastor who had many celebrities attending his church, if that's any hint:

> It seems to represent what I call the ". . . with a twist of Christianity" trend. There is mainstream culture, celebrities, fashion, music, modish political activism and a message of self-love, but with a twist of Christianity. . . . So, if Christianity is such an inessential add-on, why become a Christian? . . . Instead of making me want to become more like them, it looks very much as if they want to become more like *me*.[1]

What Sixsmith is describing—the "with a twist of Christianity" phenom—is almost verbatim what my friend Katy shared. If Christianity is just "peppered in," why not do away with Christianity altogether? The story of exclusion is the first dark dream of Evangelicalism. And what Katy is recounting is the second dark dream of many American Christians, the equal and opposite story to that of exclusion.

It's the cynical dream of *relevance*.

FLAMES, BRITNEY SPEARS, AND JESUS

When I was in high school, I had a friend I'll call Fashion Pete who was tall and good-looking and musical and fashionable, and everyone wanted to be around him. I was not fashionable, but I did have a sense of humor, so he kept me around, and we made a motley pair. Fashion Pete had a magical way of getting everyone to do the things he wanted them to do, so when he told me I should join him at his youth group one night, I said yes. This youth group was unlike anything I had experienced in my small Lutheran church growing up. The group was called Ignite, which was a metaphor for the way youth group would light all of us on fire for Jesus. The first time I walked into the parking lot, I was amazed. School buses packed with hundreds of kids came cruising in behind me, and I wondered if I'd accidentally shown up at a Britney Spears concert. They kept the church doors locked as the worship rock band practiced, and while we waited, we could play video games and pool. Sometimes we watched dirt-bike riders do huge jump tricks as if to say, "You *know* Jesus would have rolled up to Jerusalem in one of these bad boys, kids!"

Me: Yeah! Yeah, we do know! Dirt bikes! Jesus!

Also me: Wait, what's happening? Where's Britney Spears? Am I lost?

My friend Fashion Pete assured me that yes, this was youth group. Only it wasn't just youth group. It was Ignite, baby. *Wowzers. Welcome to the big leagues.*

When we walked inside, the lights were low, and for some reason there was a giant helicopter on the ceiling with a crash test dummy tumbling out of it. I asked people what the dummy and the helicopter meant, but they told me not to worry about that. At eight, a video played, telling us not to be violent or dress inappropriately, complete with examples and everything, and then the worship band kicked things off. The band was loud and upbeat. On the fourth song, the main singer cried about her love for Jesus, and I tried to cry about that, too, but I don't think I ever did. Then the speaker named Josh sprinted onstage. Josh had steely blue eyes and wore a cool shirt with flames and tigers imprinted on his shoulder. This is a genius idea, by the way, because printed T-shirts are like a bunch of noncommittal tattoos. Josh was funny, and he was really inspirational, because he talked about how God gave each of us a dream and how if we had holes in our hearts, God could fill them. I wanted to be Josh when I grew up, that much I knew. It just felt so . . . *inspiring.*

Given all the sugar consumption and adrenaline, I think from that point I was clinically hooked. The next Wednesday, I was there. Then again. And again. As a homeschooled kid from the country, this was the best thing that'd happened to me since personally reading the U.S. Constitution.

But in the following months, I noticed something didn't sit right with me, and I wondered whether other people felt it like I did. Josh's talks were great, but I couldn't remember anywhere in the Bible where God came to someone and said, "You have a dream, and I want to fulfill that dream." From what I could tell in my own sporadic reading of the Bible, it seemed more like God came to people and said things like "*I* have a dream, and whether you like it or not, it's going to happen, so you should just either help Me or go cry about it in a cave somewhere." I remember one talk Josh gave about how, in the New Testament, an angel told Elizabeth's husband that she would get pregnant with John the Baptist, and Elizabeth was happy, even though she couldn't have baby *Jesus* like her cousin Mary. Josh told us the lesson was not to be jealous of people who get more stuff, because God has plenty of stuff for all of us. I wondered if that was really the point the gospel writer Luke was trying to make with the whole Virgin Birth account, but I rolled with it because Josh was right after all. You really *shouldn't* be jealous.

I don't think Josh was intentionally deceiving people. I think he was just a really nice guy who probably should have been making good money by selling vending machines like my uncle or something. Or maybe he was just a guy who wasn't aware, like a lot of us, of how his version of the Bible was skewed by his culture. Maybe no one ever taught him God's dream, so he just made one up to be relevant. My last year of high school, two months before I went to college, I went on a mission trip to South Africa with Josh, Fashion Pete, and maybe sixty other kids from youth group. We stayed in a little village called QwaQwa and worked with some pretty cool college kids with tattoos, who were also friends with a guy from one of my favorite punk rock bands called Good Charlotte. We ate wildebeest the first night, which I wanted to object to because I knew someone killed by wildebeests—his name was Mufasa—but I kept my mouth shut and ate in little forkfuls. Really wildebeest wasn't too bad, and the whole trip was great until they asked us to do some actual work. The morning after we arrived, we rolled up to the village of QwaQwa in our rental bus. When I saw QwaQwa, something happened within me. There were no tall buildings, no vending machines, no McDonald's. I saw a large collection of little tin sheds the same size as the kind Americans keep in their back-yards for lawnmowers and garden tools. The people in the village greeted us warmly when we walked by and invited us into their homes, where they would cook chicken broth for their family's meal. They talked about not having medical care or clean water and about how a lot of their people were sick.

As we sat in these peoples' homes, I started to feel the

same way I felt at the shopping mall with Macho Man. *Why am I here? What do I have to offer these people?* I knew the other students were so excited we were teaching these poor people to be ignited for Jesus. I wasn't excited. I kept thinking about all the sermons I'd heard at Ignite. If God's goal is to fulfill people's dreams, *He must really hate these people.* Either that or God was really bad at His job. At the same time, as I talked with the people in QwaQwa, I felt like I was meeting the gentlest, most hospitable people I'd ever known. I was having a hard time figuring out why God would want to fulfill *my* dreams, as Ignite assured me, and not theirs. *Maybe they don't know about God fulfilling their dreams. Maybe they just need someone to tell them.* After a month I went home and told everyone about how great the trip was, but I couldn't shake the nagging questions.

A week after my trip to South Africa, the shallowness of Ignite hit home for me. Hard.

I was packing for college one morning, and I heard my mom scream in our backyard. I ran outside, and I saw my youngest brother, Joseph, lying on our pool deck, soaking wet. He didn't look like his normal self, with his beautiful curls and ruddy chubby cheeks. He looked pale, blue, limp. I ran and tried to resuscitate him. He didn't respond. Another of my brothers called 911. The rest is a blur. I remember sitting in my living room, trying to explain to people calling our house that I thought my brother was dead, so my mom wasn't available right now.

A week later, I was sitting at Joseph's funeral, looking at the smallest shiny white casket I'd ever seen. I sang a song about eternity for everyone. But I kept thinking, *God, if You want to fulfill people's dreams, You must really hate me and the people in Africa, because this is a* nightmare.

My best friend Fashion Pete left the church after my brother's drowning accident. He told me about some really terrible things that happened to him when he was younger and said that if God wanted to fulfill people's dreams, He was doing a real crap job of it. I couldn't blame him. Most of my friends from Ignite also left the church. Relevance is funny like that. The more relevant you are now, the less relevant you'll be in ten years. Or in a different culture. Or when life rocks you with tragedy. Nothing could have been less relevant to me than "relevance" in those few weeks.

Unlike Worldview Camp, Josh and the Ignite gang weren't mean or hostile. They were nice, and they were trying to be as inclusive as possible. They were taking what the Bible said and trying to make it relevant to everyone . . . at least, to every young American teenager whose life was going pretty well, whose shot at moving up in life was obvious, and who had the privilege of dreaming beyond chicken soup for tomorrow. They told us God wanted to show us favor, to bless us, and to give us victory for whatever dreams He had laid on our hearts. But I didn't understand, at the time, what a culturally narrow idea this was. My dreams, being an American, tended to be about better health, a bigger income, and a really big flat-screen television where I could binge the original Star Wars trilogy with my own family-sized Cheez-It box and everybody would leave me alone. Those were my dreams, and Josh was not going to argue with them. So I'm thankful Josh took us to another culture. There, I saw how irrelevant my dreams were. It wasn't too long after this that I also decided the church wasn't relevant to me after all.

I've always had a hard time explaining my relationship to Christianity during this time. I wouldn't have said I rejected it or Jesus. I read the Bible sometimes, especially the books about Jesus. I was still interested in spirituality. But I also felt out of place in the big movements around me: Relevance didn't seem especially important to me. Josh was telling me only things I could have heard at a Starbucks convention. So, as Ben Sixsmith says above, why not have all that *and* premarital sex? Exclusion just seemed mean. Both exclusion and relevance felt to me more like American projects than anything I'd heard about Jesus or His dreams. Most importantly for me at the time, neither had answers for the two most horrifying months of my life.

About a month ago, I told some of this story to an Anglican pastor friend at a coffee shop here in Indianapolis. He stopped me at this part of my story and said, "You know what you were doing at that point in your life? You were deconstructing. You just didn't have the word for it."

THE (HOLY) GHOST IN THE MACHINE

Jesus encountered another crowd during His earthly ministry—the Sadducees. Unlike the Pharisees, the Sadducees didn't try to exclude Rome. They tried to *become* Rome. "If you can't beat them," the Sadducees reasoned, "why not join them?" The Sadducees had high positions in society and were respected and honored by Roman elites. That's because they claimed they believed the Scriptures, but they shied away from the offensive parts. They didn't believe in the resurrection of the dead, and they believed humans pretty much ran the show here on earth. That meant that God's dreams for the world didn't really matter. What mattered was living your best life, here and now, whatever that was. For them, the Bible needed to be made relevant to the culture surrounding them. That's why they taught only from the first five books—Genesis through Deuteronomy. The rest, they felt, was not inspiring enough. It was irrelevant. By making their own "Bible within a Bible," the Sadducees could affirm whatever story the elites were trying to tell. The Scriptures weren't a tool for exclusion. They were a tool for *relevance* . . . at least to one particular time, place, and culture. It's interesting to me that we have lots of writings from the Pharisees of Jesus's day and long after. We have hardly any documents from the Sadducees and know little about them. The Sadducees seem to have come and gone with the Roman tide. It's not totally shocking. Their relevance wasn't relevant fifty years later, and it's not relevant today. I'll say it again: Nothing is less relevant than relevance.

When Jesus encountered the Sadducees, He criticized the way their respectable version of faith had skewed God's dreams: "You do not understand the Scriptures nor the power of God" (Matthew 22:29, NASB). Their faith was something like what Ben Sixsmith called "mainstream culture . . . with a twist of Christianity." But Jesus rejected this dream—the dark dream of relevance. And we've already heard Jesus's response: "The eye is the lamp of the body. If your eyes are healthy, your whole body will be full of light. But if your eyes are unhealthy, your whole body will be full of darkness" (Matthew 6:22–23). Immediately afterward, Jesus went on to say, "No one can serve two masters. Either you will hate the one and love the other, or you will be devoted to the one and despise the other. You cannot serve both God and money" (verse 24). This was a not-so-subtle critique of the Sadducees and the Pharisees alike. Both of them were using the Bible as a tool to gain personal power. The Pharisees were more powerful through their popularity among the people. The Sadducees wanted power among the who's who of Roman society. But at the end of the day, Jesus said neither of them were following God's dreams. They were following their own small, cynical dreams of *exclusion* and *relevance*.

Once, when theologian Dietrich Bonhoeffer visited America, he took a look around at both the conservative and liberal Protestants and decided he didn't like what he saw. In fact, he had a word to describe us: *pragmatic.*[2] I thought that was profound, especially after I looked up the word *pragmatism.* One of its key doctrines is that "truth is preeminently to be tested by the practical consequences of belief."[3] In other words, Truth is whatever works. If we don't like what the Bible says about greed, why not just make it into a book that teaches us biblical principles for leadership? Or business? If we're trying to feel a certain way about ourselves, how about we make the Bible a book about therapeutic techniques and self-help? If we want a new house, clothes, and a perfect lover? Then the Bible's just a few Instagrammable quotes about actualizing our reality by speaking it into existence. That's pragmatism. Bonhoeffer thought Americans tended to adjust the Bible to fit our personal projects. He'd already seen the dangers of that kind of thinking in the way Hitler used the Bible to promote his right-wing fascism. That, too, was pragmatism, which is why Bonhoeffer despised it in our context. As Bonhoeffer historian Reggie L. Williams put it, Bonhoeffer was disturbed to find that, "for American liberal Christians, much the same as it was in Germany, Christianity, civilization, and culture were nearly synonymous."[4] Relevance isn't Jesus's dream. Exclusion isn't Jesus's dream.

Those dreams are far too small.

Jesus's dreams are bigger. And better.

5

Vacuum

We do not draw people to Christ by loudly discrediting what they believe, by telling them how wrong they are and how right we are, but by showing them a light that is so lovely that they want with all their hearts to know the source of it.

—MADELEINE L'ENGLE, *Herself*

"Jesus was the only One that ever raised the dead," The Misfit continued, "and He shouldn't have done it. He thrown everything off balance."

—FLANNERY O'CONNOR, *A Good Man Is Hard to Find*

I sat on the University of Missouri's quad, with the six towering pillars looming overhead and the bright, warm grass beneath us. I was with some freshman students from churched backgrounds. We'd been meeting for a few weeks to talk about the basics of Christian faith. This week, I decided to ask them an impromptu question.

"What is the gospel?" I asked. "How would you define it?" There was a long pause as thoughts of childhood Sunday schools swirled in their heads. I could tell they were trying to be careful, to use the right words in the right way.

"We're sinners," said one girl. "God became a man in Jesus, and He died to save us from our sin so that we could go to heaven."

"Okay," I said. "There's some good stuff in there. Thank you." I glanced at the other two. "What do you think?" They nodded along, afraid to rock the boat. One girl had already offered herself as tribute, so there was no need for further bloodshed. "Anything to add?" No. I've asked this question a few times to my students from Christian backgrounds. I'm pretty confident by now that the answer above is the one I'll get. It's the answer *I* would have given in elementary or high school.

"Growing up," I told them, "I thought Christianity basically meant that if God asked me to recite Luther's Small Catechism when I died, and I did, He would say, 'Good job, now you can be in heaven.' But because I was really into the arts—film, literature, music—this story never sat right with me. The ending didn't seem to follow from the beginning. Sure, the story had some poignant moments. It had romance and tension. Jesus's daring rescue of us on the cross and His resurrection always struck me as the greatest climax and resolve of any story I'd read. But what came before (whatever that was) and what came after never really matched the beauty of that moment. And the ending of the story—'now we can go to heaven'—always felt like a lame duck. Terrifying, even. It meant that nothing I cared about now mattered. It was like Christianity, for all of its beauty, actually closed the door to the world around me."

They gave me a lot of blank stares. I don't think they were sure they could agree with me. Maybe I had set too many rhetorical traps for them in the past. I needed to work on that. I continued, "This story touched my heart, for sure. I understood God's love for me, through His Son, Jesus. Not every church teaches about God's free gift of love, so I'm thankful Evangelicalism did. But what I couldn't understand was God's *plan* for me. It felt like God and I were on two different tracks: He's got heaven covered. I've got earth. Someday, He'll cancel everything I ever did and take me to be with Him. But I needed this story to give me a vision for life *now*. I wanted to have some kind of mission that was more than 'help other people get off this sinking ship with you.' But I couldn't see one. For example, what does that story have to do with the homework you did today, the problems you see in society, your future careers? Nothing. In fact, this story makes us cynical about life, because it tells us none of it matters in the end."

One girl was nodding. Another offered a polite rebuttal, "But we could use all these jobs to tell other people about Jesus."

"That's true," I said. "We could do that, and we should. But be honest with me. Does the news you're sharing with other people really feel like *good news* to you? Are you excited about the future of the world? Your life? Eternity? Or let me put it this way: Does your faith make the world more colorful to you or more dull? Does your Christianity open the door to life or close it? Does this version of faith give you an exciting, holistic vision for your life right now? Or does it make your life mostly meaningless, other than when you're evangelizing?"

"To be honest," one girl offered, "it feels mostly meaningless."

I know what you're thinking: *I'm glad this guy isn't my pastor.* But my point wasn't to harass these poor freshmen. It definitely wasn't to suggest that we should be standing over Scripture and judging it. My point was to invite these students into the bigger story Scripture is telling. The story evangelicals tell isn't a false story; it's just an incomplete one. It doesn't offer us hope or meaning, and we literally can't exist without those things. Something has to fill that vacuum.

What's filled the evangelical vacuum in the past fifty years are the cynical stories: exclusion and relevance.

ON ASSESSING PLYWOOD

We called our grandpa Grumpy. I'm not sure why. He was very nice, and he was only grumpy when you tried to change the television channel from Bob Vila to Nickelodeon. Or you could make him grumpy if you wanted one of his cold glass Pepsis down in the basement refrigerator. He'd need to open it for you with the bottle opener, and you'd have to step over the spiky red mats downstairs in your socks. Then Grumpy would twist the cap off the bottle, glare at you, and let out a low growl. Other than that, I don't think he was grumpy in the least. If he was, it was probably because he was my grandma's third husband, and it maybe took him a minute to warm up to *also* being *my* third grandpa.

When I was about ten years old, he called my mom to invite me, my brother, and my father to his annual builders' convention. Grumpy was a reputable contractor, and I didn't know what an annual builders' convention was, but I did know I was not good at building things. I was picturing having to look at lots of samples of wood, like oak and hickory and poison sumac, and also at roof shingles. I imagined having to murmur and nod as if one roof shingle really stood out to me among all the shingles. And I would have to say things like "This one's poison sumac. Avoid it at all costs if you can, that's what I think." It all made me nervous since I didn't know anything about wood or roof shingles. I wasn't even sure if poison sumac counted as wood. Maybe it was more of a plant, anyway. I started to form the words *No, thanks* when my mother dropped the bomb: "There will be dinner."

"Okay, I'll go! I love Grumpy just that much, Ma."

"Okay, just so you know," she said, giving me the side-eye

for my quick change of tone, "it's a big deal. Make sure to thank Grumpy for inviting you. It's a really nice event, and he can only bring a few guests every year." Once my mom explained this, I understood that the invitation meant a lot to Grumpy, even if it didn't mean a lot to me. For purely sentimental reasons, I felt honored. It was one of the first times I realized my step-grumpy really cared about me.

"Sure, I will."

"Okay, then. You'll need to dress up and everything," she said, as if this was some kind of casual throw-in.

"Dress up and everything." Those words were like a death knell to my ten-year-old ears. I pictured myself walking around in suspenders with my hair slicked back and a little monocle like one of those Charlie McCarthy ventriloquist dolls. When the builders' convention night arrived the next week, I was dragging my feet. I waited until the last possible minute to shower, paste my hair, button my slacks, and put on a crocodile grin. My social anxiety was skyrocketing. In a panic about the wood samples, I started trying to list all the kinds of trees I knew about: oak, pine, hickory, poison sumac . . . no, *not* poison sumac. *Remember, dummy? Why did I ever sign up for this?* I remembered the time my grandpa asked me for a socket wrench and I had to try four different tools before he snatched the socket wrench off the tool bench for himself. Now I was going to be stuck at a table with a lot of old men talking about the time they saved a building project by using a two-by-four instead of a four-by-four or something, and I would have to try and think of a similar story: "Oh yeah, one time I built a sandcastle with no moat. Let me tell you, it was a disaster. A real nightmare. My buddy Scotty could tell you stories, but we don't talk about it." *Remember to pause for laughter here.*

After squeezing into my old dress clothes and cleaning up, I piled into the pickup truck with my dad and brother. My dad was wearing a tie and smelled like Big Red cinnamon gum. Even if I didn't like dressing up, I liked it when he did. It was like seeing the glory of some Greek god finally unveiled or a knight donning armor—or like I was finally being let into some shared secret between grown-ups. It gave me a feeling of safety and respect, and I started to wonder if maybe—just maybe—my expectations about having to carry the conversation with building contractors was more of an anxiety-induced delusion.

We pulled up to a large white building. Hundreds of other trucks were streaming into the parking lot. Butterflies for me. When we walked inside, a stubby man with glasses offered to take our coats. I had planned to hang mine on the back of my chair, but my dad said, "No, it's not that kind of dinner." *Not that kind of dinner? What kind of dinner is it? I hope it's the food kind.* I gave the man my coat, and we entered the banquet hall.

I gasped.

The hall was decorated with beautiful swan ice sculptures sitting atop white tablecloths set with ornate plates and glasses. I could smell the Sterno cans adding their delicate heat to exotic foods I didn't know were edible, like elk, bison, and venison sausage. We sat down at our reserved seats, and I looked at Grumpy as though he were just another walking god—with his six-foot-five frame towering over everyone—as he made small talk. As it turned out, the only interest anyone paid to me was an invitation to flick straw wads through finger field goals. Nobody asked me about roof shingles or wood samples. After a bit, the waiters delivered the food. I'd never had a meal brought to me one course at a time, so at first I felt disappointed that dinner was only a side salad. Then the next course came, and the next and the next: elk meatballs, bacon-wrapped stuffed jalapeños, venison cheese dip, chocolate eclairs . . . I started to wonder if maybe contracting *was,* after all, an ideal career for a guy like me.

As dessert was served, someone stood up onstage, took the microphone, and said a lot of nice things about contracting and made some jokes about his wife I didn't understand. Then he introduced the guest speaker for the night . . . my longtime Detroit Red Wings hockey hero and a legend, Gordie Howe. He told stories about being a pro hockey player in the 1960s as I clung to his every word. Then, after the dinner, my dad offered to take me to see Gordie. I followed in a trance as we approached him, and I nearly puked with nervousness as Gordie gave me his autograph in his new book, (*And . . . Howe!*), and also a noogie on the head. And I still have that noogie to this very day.

It was one of the greatest nights of my life.

A few years later, when Grumpy invited me to the builders' convention again, I wasn't just touched by his gesture; I was genuinely *excited.* I was ready, with my hair combed and my newly pressed shirt tucked, hours before the convention started. I skipped breakfast and lunch in anticipation of the delicious meal ahead. I would have been happy to spend my own allowance to go, but Grumpy had already paid my way. It was exciting. It was the same invitation as years before. Now, however, my experience of the invitation was different. Grumpy's loving gesture wasn't the gesture of an out-of-touch older gentleman. Now that I understood the dream behind the invitation, I was excited to live into that dream. The hope of another dreamy night under chandeliers changed the way I went about my day, my week even. I wasn't just touched.

It transformed me.

I once showed up at a church in an old tweed suit that a friend gave me. It was a fancy church, and I was embarrassed. A guy in front of me made a comment about my suit, and then I felt even more embarrassed, so I tried to explain it by saying it was given to me by my older friend who served as a spy in the Cold War, to add a little interest. The man gave me a puzzled look and said, "How touching." I later asked my wealthy friend if that was a rich person dis. She said, "Oh yes. It was *definitely* a rich person dis."

That, I think, is how many of us feel about the evangelical version of the gospel. We're touched by it, but we really have no idea what it means. Out of His incredible love, our heavenly Father sent His Son to die on the cross for us. That's amazing—so much so that I wrote a whole book about it (*Faker*).[1] But if we understand only that part of the Bible's story, it's a bit like hearing, "Your grandpa bought you expensive tickets to the builders' convention," when we have no idea what a builders' convention is. It's a message that has the power to touch our hearts, but not to transform our everyday lives. As the author of Proverbs put it, "Where there is no vision, the people are unrestrained" (29:18, NASB).

We evangelicals understand the *sentiment* of the gospel, but we don't understand the *vision* of the gospel. That's why, growing up, I heard lots of sermons that went something like this:

> Okay, Jesus has a lot of great ideas for things we could be doing in the world, but let's be real; we're never going to do any of those things. So it's a good thing we have Jesus. The end.

This kind of preaching gave me the impression that there were only two moments that mattered in my life:

Moment 1: The day I learned the definition of justification by faith alone

Moment 2: The day I arrived at the pearly gates and God
asked me to recite the definition of justification by faith
alone

I am, to be clear, *profoundly* thankful for the truth that
Jesus's righteousness is my righteousness. I'm so glad I didn't
grow up in a church that taught I needed to do certain things
to make God happy with me. I'm so glad to have learned,
early on, that the gospel is all about Jesus's mercy, not my
good works. It's all grace. All mercy. All the time. I treasure
these truths every day.

But it was all a bit like hearing the first movement of a
symphony, then shutting off the song. Or telling the opening
of a story, then closing the book. I couldn't understand how
those two moments had anything to do with all the moments
in my life between them. What did these things have to do
with anything I cared about? Art? Literature? Music? Friend-
ships? When I left the church at eighteen, it didn't feel like I
was rebelling against Christianity. It just felt like I was taking
Christianity to its logical conclusion. In my understanding of
faith, the Christian story had absolutely nothing to do with
the world I lived in. So why not just cash in on that doctrinal
knowledge when I reach the pearly gates and take the rest
into my own hands?

Then I met C. S. Lewis.

During my last two semesters in college, I traveled abroad
to study creative writing and literature at Oxford University.
It had been three years since I seriously attended church. I
still considered myself a post-Bible, post-religion Christian
who was more into spirituality and the life of Jesus than what
we called Christianity in America. During my first semester at
Oxford, I took some tutorials about early children's literature, one of them focusing on British author C. S. Lewis. My

tutor suggested I read several biographies of Lewis. For Lewis, formerly an atheist, coming to faith in Christ was less about understanding rigorous arguments, though there was some of that. It was more about understanding the way the Bible gave us space to *dream*. For Lewis, joy wasn't a feeling. It was an "inconsolable longing" for a "far-off country" yet to come. *It was a compelling vision.* Christianity was the only vision of life that explained and encouraged us to explore that joyful feeling. Lewis said,

> In speaking of this desire for our own far-off country . . . I am trying to rip open the inconsolable secret in each one of you—the secret which hurts so much that you take your revenge on it by calling it names like Nostalgia and Romanticism and Adolescence; the secret also which pierces with such sweetness. . . . These things—the beauty, the memory of our own past—are good images of what we really desire; but if they are mistaken for the thing itself, they turn into dumb idols, breaking the hearts of their worshippers. For they are not the thing itself; they are only the scent of a flower we have not found, the echo of a tune we have not heard, news from a country we have never yet visited.[2]

Up until this point, Christianity had closed the door to my deepest longings. But for Lewis, atheism and other religions killed our deep, long-forgotten dreams about love, freedom, and beauty. The Christian vision—the way he described it—swung the door open to the world rather than shut it. In a later essay, he wrote about how Christianity gave him the only framework he could find for believing in true love, true freedom, and true beauty:

> Christian theology can fit in science, art, morality, and the sub-Christian religions. The scientific point of view cannot

fit in any of these things, not even science itself. I believe in Christianity as I believe that the Sun has risen, not only because I see it, but because by it I see everything else.[3]

According to Lewis, the Christian vision helps us access the world we already inhabit in new and profound ways. Christianity dares us to desire. It dares us to dream. I didn't know Christians could feel that erotic kind of way about life, the way I felt. Not only could we, argued Lewis, but Jesus says we *must*. This was new to me: What if Jesus, as Lewis noted, found our desires not too strong but too weak? What if Jesus wasn't the enemy of my deepest, most profound dreams?

What if Jesus came to *restore* them?

SLOUCHING TOWARD JERUSALEM

Imagine we are Israelite slaves, back in Egypt. Yahweh comes to us promising to fulfill our dream to be a free, loving, beautiful community in our Promised Land. Up until this point, Pharaoh has been a real tool, so Yahweh makes him a little something the Mafia like to call "an offer he can't refuse": Yahweh will take the life of every firstborn child of Pharaoh's, just like Pharaoh had taken the lives of Israelite children for decades. Everyone who wants to escape can, by painting the blood of a lamb over their doorway, telling the angel of death to pass by.

Let's say after the Israelites are spared from the curse of the angel of death, Moses knocks on everyone's door and says, "Okay, time to go to the Promised Land!"

The people say, "Well, I think we will stay here because, see, we were already rescued by the blood of the lamb. Besides, Egypt just got cable television." So Moses waits outside, checking his watch, wondering when the Israelites will realize Pharaoh wants to kill them. But as the day wears on, everyone is still inside watching cable television. Finally, feeling a little frustrated, Moses swings open an Israelite family's door in a huff. He's happy to see a few Israelites gathered together to study theology.

"Perfect!" says one Israelite. "Moses, we had a question for you. We were just reading about the blood of the lamb and were wondering how this all worked. Are we now free from the angel of death?"

"Absolutely!" says Moses. "You are free from the curse of death. Praise God! The lamb of God saved you. So let's pack our bags and get moving, because the Red Sea is at low tide and I really would prefer not to be hedged against it when Pharaoh's schizophrenia medication wears off." But the Israelites look at him like he's from Mars or something.

"But . . . where are we going? I thought we were rescued from the angel of death."

"Yes! Yes, God rescued you, so you can follow Him! He has a dream for you. You don't have to be a slave in Egypt anymore. You can be free, and you can go to a land flowing with milk and honey!" They look at one another like Moses is still from Mars and now he is speaking Martian.

"Will there be baseball?" one asks.

"Baseball? Yes, sure. I don't know."

"Will there be Cracker Jack?"

"What? Yes. Cracker Jack, lots of Cracker Jack, with little prizes and everything."

"Cats?"

"You're missing the point. The point is you have a purpose, a mission, a dream. Why are you sitting around?"

Stony silence.

"Well," one says, "it sounds like salvation by works, Moses. Don't you understand the doctrine of justification by faith alone? Are you saying the blood of the lamb didn't *actually* save us from God's judgment?"

"*Of course* it did," says Moses. "But don't you remember what He rescued you *for*? You know how I wrote that God heard your cries and decided to rescue you from slavery *in order to bring you into the land He would show you*?[4] Don't you remember He rescued you because He remembered His promise to Abraham, that He would bless the nations through you?[5] Yes, He rescued you *from* the angel of death. He wants to make you into a loving, just, beautiful community. He wants to care for the earth and the poor and the widow and the orphan through you. He wants to bring healing to the nations and restore the world back to the way it's supposed to be *through you*. He wants you to give other people a picture of God's reign *through you,* here and now! Isn't that exciting?"

"Hmm," says another. "That sounds like a social gospel. You've got weird ideas, Moses. You should stop being so political and stick to being a pastor or a shepherd or a prophet or whatever you are."

"Yeah," says another. "We really need to get back to our Bible studies."

You get the point. If Israel was rescued from death but didn't follow God's dream, they might as well have stayed slaves. Rescue from God's judgment was the beginning of their story, not the end. The same is true of us.

Yes, the Lamb of God—Jesus—rescued us from God's judgment. But there's *more to the story*. We've been invited out of slavery to sin and into something else: God's dreams. If we don't follow them, we're like the slaves sitting in their Egyptian houses, still wrapped in chains, doing our Bible studies. The offer of Jesus's free rescue is great news. But if we can't answer the question "What's He rescuing us *for*?"

we don't have a very compelling offer. We're like people with free builders' convention tickets . . . who have no idea what a builders' convention is. The offer of the gospel isn't *less* than a free ticket to the builders' convention. But it's so much more.

It's no wonder we're stuck in the cynical dreams of exclusion and relevance. We've never been taught another dream exists.

It's time to recover the vision behind the rescue: God's dreams.

PART 2

RESTORATION

6

Escape

I despise that religion that can carry Bibles to the heathen
on the other side of the globe and withhold them from heathen on this side—which can talk about human rights yon-
der and traffic in human flesh here.
—FREDERICK DOUGLASS, "American Slavery," 1847

How can any one remain interested in a religion which
seems to have no concern with nine-tenths of his life?
—DOROTHY L. SAYERS, "The Secular Vocation
Is Sacred" from *Creed or Chaos*

Growing up, I thought God wanted everyone to go to His
party, called heaven, because He was vaguely mad at all
of us for enjoying earth too much. So, I figured we all just
kind of had to deal with God not liking our world, and if we
wanted to get on His good side, we had to at least pretend to
want to go to this magical play place He created called heaven.
Don't get me wrong; heaven was . . . *fine.* It was like earth,
except that there was no television or macaroni and cheese,
and there was nothing to do except sing in a long trance always, all the time, and if someone asked how my day was
going, I might say, "Well, I'm just sort of floating around
today. And you?"

"Yeah, I'm floating around, just like I do always, all the
time."

"Cool, cool, cool. I've got a float-around with Noah at three. I was going to ask him about the dinosaurs."

"Oh gosh, don't even. He's so sick of answering that one. I'll give you my notes. Choir's about to start!"

In that sense, having a relationship with God felt like having a relationship with a rich gothic friend who invited you to his mansion so he could fold his arms and stare at you from a dark corner in the room while you pretended to enjoy all the pretty things he'd collected and made polite conversation about his hobbies like bloodbaths, altars, and legal codes concerning skin disease. Also the doors were locked so you would have to be his friend forever.

I don't know why I thought this way about God's future exactly. Maybe it was from hearing evangelicals talking about "going to heaven" and leaving me to fill in the blanks. Or maybe it was easier to picture God's vision that way because then I didn't have to take it too seriously. I do know that somehow most evangelicals' first impression of God's vision for our future seems similar to mine.

Take a student named Michael. Michael sat down with me a few years ago and said he did not want to be a Christian anymore. I asked him why, and he told me it was because if he was a Christian, he couldn't like pretty girls.

"But God made pretty girls," I said. "What's wrong with liking pretty girls?" He said it sounded too worldly, and he had been taught he needed to give up worldly things for Jesus. He said he would also have to give up his painting if he truly loved Jesus, even though painting made him feel alive.

"But God is creative," I said. "He created the world. What's wrong with your painting? That seems godly to me." We took a long walk around campus, and he shared with me about growing up in a church that taught him his sports, hobbies, and sense of humor were all problems. They were getting in the way of his faith because they were keeping him from doing the real work of Christians: helping to grow his youth group. This, his youth leader explained, is what Jesus meant by "dying to self" and "taking up your cross and following me." Do more churchy things. Focus on heaven. Do things that will last, and here's the list:

1. Evangelize.
2. Go to church.
3. Pray.

As we walked to one of Michael's favorite spots in Columbia—a parking-garage rooftop with a beautiful view of the entire city—we both stared silently at the fall trees popping with brilliant orange and fiery red leaves.

"I don't think the God who made all this wants you to hate the world you live in," I said. "It's true that the Bible warns about worldliness. But worldliness isn't the same as *earthiness.* You were made to be earthy. That's what it means to be human. Worldliness is about participating in the patterns and systems that bring harm and destruction to others and the earth we live in. In that sense, not caring about the world is kind of . . . *worldly.*"

Michael stared at me like I was speaking Swahili.

"Okay, let me put it this way." I tried again. "Don't you delight in your paintings?"

He nodded, thinking.

"The world you live in is God's painting. There are so many beautiful things in this world inspired by God—music, art, sports, and, yes, male and female beauty. Why do you think God would be disappointed in you for enjoying His painting and wanting to make more things like it?"

"Well, that makes sense," he said. "But it seems like if we're all going to heaven anyway, none of that matters."

"You're right," I said. "But let me ask you this, Michael.

Where in the Bible can you find the phrase *going to heaven*?"
He thought for a minute.

"I can't remember," he said.

"That's right," I said. "That's because it's *not in there.*"

"But isn't that the whole point of being a Christian?"

"Well, if it is, we have a big problem: God doesn't love us."
He looked at me, shocked. "We're embodied creatures, Michael. So if God doesn't love our bodies or the earthy things we love, we can't really say He loves *us*. We humans are creatures, by definition. So I guess my real question for you, Michael, is . . . do you think God loves *you*? I mean, the whole you? Your interests? Your hobbies? Your body? Your personality?"

"Definitely not," he said, and tears filled his eyes. "I don't think anyone at church meant to tell me that, but that's sort of what I got out of the whole experience."

"Yeah," I said. "I know exactly what you mean."

THE DAY MY PASTOR CANCELED JESUS

Back when I interviewed for the job in the trailer park church, the pastor said my fiancée, Brenna, would need to quit school. It was a waste of time, he said, compared with helping me spread the gospel. I said that I didn't think it was a waste of time and that she wouldn't be quitting school.

He said, "Okay, fine."

But two months after I accepted the job, the pastor marched into my office. He said, "If Brenna doesn't quit her education this week, you can't work here anymore."

"But we agreed she wouldn't have to do that," I said.

"Well, she does. I'm the pastor here, and that's what I say. If she doesn't, you're fired."

"But that means we'll have thousands of dollars of debt with nothing to show for it," I said.

"We'll help pay the tuition. We have a fund for that kind of thing." It wasn't much of a choice. If I lost my job, Brenna would have to quit school anyway. It was the first time I'd ever been blackmailed . . . and it was by a *pastor*. Worse than that, now I was stuck in this job with no way out.

As it turns out, that was by design. It kept our mouths shut. Or at least, it was supposed to.

One Sunday a few months later, the pastor preached to us about God's dream for America. He told us the world is like a sinking ship and "our job is to throw life preservers to people so they can escape this ship, not to polish the brass on the *Titanic*!" He also explained how the book of Revelation was about Russian helicopters nuking America because we had so many liberals in our country. I thought the polishing brass part was funny and also the Russian helicopters, but I wasn't sure they were supposed to be. The pastor went on to complain that *some* people wanted to do good things for our community, like starting reading tutorships and helping feed people, and *some* people were wasting their time because the point of church is to get people saved so they'll go to heaven. I wondered at what point in the sermon he would start reading off my license plate number.

Now, you might wonder how the pastor squared that with all of Jesus's teaching. As the sermon went on, so did I. That's when the pastor told us exactly how he would do that. Toward the end of his sermon, the pastor announced that he was *canceling Jesus*.

Yes, that's right. He said we weren't allowed to teach Jesus's words anymore. These four Gospel accounts, he said, seemed too concerned with our earthly lives. Christianity, on the other hand, was obviously a story about escape, which we obviously could do by raising our hands, praying a prayer, and signing up for an eternity away in a place called heaven.

The problem was, the pastor couldn't find anything in Jesus's teaching that talked about this story. In fact, Jesus seemed to teach the *opposite*. Jesus taught that God's heavenly kingdom was invading earth: "Your kingdom come, your will be done, on earth as it is in heaven" (Matthew 6:10). Jesus seemed really concerned about "worldly" things like justice, mercy, love, freedom, caring for the poor, standing for the abused, and loving our neighbors.

So, the pastor concluded that Jesus didn't understand Christianity.

Because of that, no one at this church was allowed to teach from the four Gospels anymore. *Jesus was canceled.* Can you imagine one of the New Testament apostles stumbling on this church?

PAUL: Okay, Church, give us an update.

CHURCH: Love your work, Paul. Great stuff. Big fan. Especially the Romans Road.

PAUL: The what now?

CHURCH: The Romans Road! You know, where we jump back and forth throughout your letter to teach people the true gospel?

PAUL: Okay . . . I did mean that to be read from beginning to end, you know. But whatever. As long as you're faithful to the teaching handed down to you in the life and teachings of Jesus.

CHURCH: Actually we helped clear things up. We don't even use the four Gospels. Those have a bunch of confusing things about caring for the poor and stuff.

PAUL: That's not confusing.

CHURCH: Well, it is if you don't want to do it.

PAUL: Are you serious? I'm away for two thousand years and you cancel *Jesus*?

CHURCH: Yeah, He doesn't really fit with the true gospel
   of Christianity.
PAUL: Jesus is literally the whole point of Christianity.
CHURCH: Mmm, I don't think so.
PAUL: You'll be getting a letter from my boss.

The day after the sermon, I knocked on the pastor's door
to ask a few questions about his theology. The more questions I asked, the more agitated the pastor became. After a
bit, I left awkwardly. Later that afternoon, I received a short
phone call from the pastor.

"Nick, look, it's not going to work out. We need to let you
go. We'll take care of you, though, until you find something
else. Don't worry. We'll do that much for you because we love
you. I just wish you were more teachable, that's all."

More teachable? I wondered what that word meant to him.
Maybe it meant I would start calling him "Dr. Jones" like
people at his church did . . . even though the pastor had only
an undergraduate education from a Bible college. I decided
whatever "teachable" was, I was glad I wasn't that.

The next Friday, I walked into the office to collect a paycheck from the secretary.

"By the way," she said, "the pastor told me to let you know
this is the only paycheck you'll be getting from us."

"But he said he'd take care of us until we found something."

"Oh, he told me you *had* found something."

"No, I haven't." She paused, and her lip trembled a little.
"So are you guys still planning on helping us pay Brenna's
tuition bills? The ones the pastor promised to help us with
when he forced her to quit school?" She shook her head.

"I'm sorry, no," she said. "That's what the pastor told me."

The point of telling you this isn't so you can be mad at this pastor or this church. I spent a long time being mad at them, and there's a place for that. In fact, I learned during this time that the Bible has all kinds of great psalms if you have a hankering for praying that oppressive men be pillaged, burned, humiliated, stripped naked, beheaded, scorched, choked by their own food, imprisoned in chains of their own making, deserted in the wilderness, blotted out of history, seized by debt collectors, made to eat their own feces, and other interesting forms of poetic justice. I'd never known how relevant all these prayers were. They were great.

But as I said, that's not the point of this story. This experience, for me, was a personal revelation. I saw the real implications of the theology of escape. It's a story that says, "Your body, emotions, money, and personality don't ultimately matter to God, because heaven." If the Bible was, as the pastor once said, "Basic Instructions Before Leaving Earth" (BIBLE, get it?), then let's just admit it—the pastor was 100 percent justified in taking advantage of me, my young wife, and the trailer park community surrounding us. So long as he was getting our souls saved, nothing else mattered. He was free to continue eating steak dinners at restaurants every night (as he did), free to spend thousands of the church's dollars on trips to country shows in Branson, Missouri, and free to employ "spiritually gifted" sex offenders on staff, all while watching the community around him burn. It was the natural logic to the story of escape: None of this matters. It'll all be burned anyway, so we might as well start now. Heaven, after all, is our goal.

What I learned from this experience is that the story of escape will always lead to the logic of abuse.

At least this pastor *admitted* Jesus didn't fit into this story.

The trailer park church deepened my understanding of evangelical culture. Having grown up believing the story of escape, I can tell you it makes perfect sense—according to this story—that a pastor would take advantage of the people in his congregation and community. That is the logic of escape playing out. It makes perfect sense that when a presidential candidate comes along saying, "I'll help you get what's yours!" evangelicals are on him like church ladies on a casserole. It fits perfectly with the story of escape. And it's not surprising to me that all this climaxed in an insurrection at the Capitol.

It's what our dreams made.

But it wasn't always this way. Evangelicalism wasn't always this way. We American Evangelicals were dreamers, once.

EVANGELICALS AS ESCAPE ARTISTS

Evangelicalism in the eighteenth century was a far cry from the Evangelicalism we see today. As historian Richard Lovelace has put it, nineteenth-century evangelicals were "united in working and praying toward spiritual, cultural and social renewal."[1] Andrew Wilson summarized the ways Evangelicalism revolutionized the world for good:

> Indeed, the changes within Western Christianity in this period—great awakenings and evangelical revivals, . . . the religious Enlightenment, the rise of abolitionism, hymn writing, the modern missions movement, and many others—are so numerous and varied that it would take a whole book just to summarize them.[2]

Indeed. In fact, many of the causes evangelicals consider "liberal" agendas today were started by these nineteenth-century *evangelicals.* In her book *The Evangelical Imagination,* Karen Swallow Prior wrote,

It was in large part owing to the early evangelicals that the larger society began to see human suffering in a different way—as a result of systemic injustices that could and should be eased. . . . They therefore set out to abolish the slave trade, educate the poor, improve conditions for laborers, and stem cruelty to animals.[3]

None of these were seen as compromises to the inerrancy of Scripture or the doctrine of justification. But there's one key underlying difference between the Evangelicalism of then and the Evangelicalism of today: In the early nineteenth century, Evangelicalism had clear ties to the Protestant Reformation. It proclaimed a gospel not of escape but of Jesus bringing renewal to all things.

The Civil War changed that. After the Civil War, America—and the church—had been torn in two. Arguments over how (or whether) to restore what was stolen from Black Americans abounded. At the same time, a small sect of separatist teachers led by John Darby, who had defected from the Anglican church—citing his own private reading of Scripture—began to teach a brand-new, never-before-seen system of doctrine. Darby believed the Old Testament was concerned with earthly realities, but the New Testament—and therefore the church today—was concerned only with spiritual realities: "Whenever then we turn to what is Jewish . . . we have the principle of apostasy in us."[4] Darby taught that everything "earthly" was going to burn away in a great and terrible "tribulation," another innovative teaching. At this time, the church would be "raptured" into heaven.[5] Therefore, believers shouldn't concern themselves at all with earthly realities but rather focus on winning souls to Christ. In fact, Darby took his assertions even further, proclaiming that the entire institutional church had been apostate since the early days of the church fathers, positioning himself and his followers as the only true faithful elect.[6] Recognizing the cult-like characteristics of this movement, the vast majority of Protestants rejected Darby's teachings. This all occurred prior to the Civil War.

Even historians who wish to add nuance and complexity to the understanding of Darby readily acknowledge that he showed very little concern for the "earthly" realities surrounding him, both personally and in his roles as a pastor: the Civil War, the great Potato Famine—which greatly affected his friends and family—and so on.[7] This, of course, follows directly from Darby's overly spiritualized theology. But it was this very lack of concern for "earthly" realities that led D. L. Moody—a young, charismatic evangelist—to see in Darby's views an opportunity. What was the appeal of Darby to Moody, exactly? Simply this: Moody saw in Darby's outlook a way to unite the Northern and Southern White church after the Civil War.[8] If Jesus did not care about "earthly" realities, then discussions about reconstruction—specifically economic justice for the Black church—could be relegated to a "worldly" concern. The church (and he meant the White church) could focus on its true mission: evangelizing people to help them escape the earth. A very popular hymn created at the time typifies this vibe:

Turn your eyes upon Jesus,
Look full in His wonderful face,
And the things of earth will grow strangely dim,
In the light of His glory and grace.[9]

It's a hymn we sang every single week at the trailer park church. And yet this sentiment would have been unrecognizable to early Protestant evangelicals. That's because the god the escapist evangelicals invented was a god *against* creation and culture. His desire was to help people escape the earth and their own bodies. That meant intellectual pursuits, culture, artistic endeavors, and political engagement were all to be viewed with skepticism and even hostility. Most conveniently, calls for justice could now be safely dismissed as "worldly" concerns. Now evangelism itself, rather than being a call to discipleship, became what Christian martyr Dietrich Bonhoeffer called an offer of "cheap grace":[10] Raise your hand, pray a prayer, assent to the doctrines, and go on your merry way assured of eternity in heaven. Being a Christian, after all, had nothing to do with following the radical, earthy man named Jesus. Evangelicalism, which just fifty years before spearheaded the cause for abolition, now had a framework for treating such causes with suspicion and contempt. This was more than a serious vibe change. The *escapist evangelicals* had, in a sense, an entirely different DNA from the *historic Protestant evangelicals.*

Following Darby, Moody and his followers believed that the earthly realities around us were going to grow increasingly evil. "I find that the earth," said Moody, "is to grow worse and worse and that at length there is going to be a separation (of the saved from the unsaved)."[11] As clergyman and social reformer Henry Ward Beecher reported, "He [Moody] thinks it is no use to attempt to work for this world. In his opinion it is blasted—a wreck bound to sink—and the only thing that is worth doing is to get as many of the crew off as you can, and let her go."[12] Now, rather than hope, escapist evangelicals began to anticipate—and fear—the inevitable downward spiral of the world. Not only was civilization going to collapse, Moody believed, but eventually the church would collapse with it, resulting in the great tribulation.

This created an entirely new set of instincts in evangelicals after 1905, when the incredibly popular Scofield Bible spread the escapist evangelical viewpoint like wildfire, promoting fear, cynicism, and separatism. The crowd calling themselves "evangelicals" were no longer a hopeful, socially engaged movement. The vibe of escapist Evangelicalism was now *fearful separatism.* As Richard Lovelace observed, the movement was now

> evangelistically active but socially passive. This outlook expected the world to become increasingly corrupt and conceived of the church's main duty as witnessing to the justifying work of Christ, not making disciples whose growth in sanctification could change the world. The result was an outlook which accurately predicted the apostasy of Western Christendom in the twentieth century but which may also have helped produce it.[13]

After nineteen hundred years of proclaiming God's growing kingdom, the escapist evangelicals changed the story. Lovelace's final line about this antisocial gospel is chilling: "The result was an outlook which accurately predicted the apostasy of Western Christendom in the twentieth century *but which may also have helped produce it.*" Lovelace is asking, What if the cynical story escapist evangelicals started telling was a self-fulfilling prophecy? What if the escapist evangelicals' fearful, cynical, antisocial "gospel" *helped cause* the Great Dechurching we're seeing today? For me, this isn't a question. It's a reality I see daily.

Now, you may wonder, *Wait. If the problem with American Evangelicalism is this escapist theology, then what about the cynical dreams of exclusion and relevance? Aren't these movements promoting just the opposite of escapism?* Great point. I believe the story of escape is the Big Cynical Story that *directly leads to* the smaller cynical dreams of exclusion and relevance.

Why? Because the *escapist vision of life is impossible to live out consistently*. Think of it this way. Imagine you're in a beautiful room. Now someone you trust very much tells you, "Nothing in this room matters." You believe them. "Nothing in this room matters." Also, the person says, "Not only does this room not matter, but it's all going to get worse and worse until one day, you escape the room just before it collapses." You believe them. The problem is, as a human being, you *enjoy* the beautiful room, which you now feel a little guilty about. You also *need* the room—you need to eat its food, sleep in its corridors, look out its windows. You're using the room for your own survival, but you're not blessing it, serving it, or caring for it in any significant way. Why would you? Nothing in the room matters, and it's all destined for destruction anyway, so it's inconceivable that somehow you should care about it, for its own sake, or work to develop it in any way. Also you are pretty bored, because living in a meaningless room is boring. So when someone enters the room, telling you a compelling and even entertaining story *about* the room—a cable news voice or podcaster or politician—you're *going* to latch on to that story. You just are. That's because you're human.

In the same way, the escapist story says, "Nothing in this world matters." But then we *need* to go on acting like things matter because we're earthly creatures, so we carry on doing our jobs and enjoying movies and managing budgets all with a vague feeling of guilt and resignation. We humans *need* a mission and a compelling narrative to live out of. The story of escape offers neither. It leaves a vacuum in our humanity, ready to be filled with anything that promises a clear story and mission. So when the snake-oil salesmen of the exclusion movement and the relevance movement sweep in, telling us that the Christian vision of our lives is about recovering

American greatness or achieving our dreams or finding a theological justification for progressive politics . . . we fall for it. Our "Christian mission" shrinks to the size of our own preferred form of self-preservation: exclusion or relevance.

But here's the good news: The story of escape is not—and has never been—the Christian vision of life.

Not by a long shot.

MARCION

The historical roots of the escapist gospel most modern evangelicals believe today may feel surprising to you, like it was to me when I first learned of the shift. But, as the early church would tell you, there's nothing new under the sun.

In the early church, there were a few charismatic leaders who had some wild ideas about Jesus. One of them was a guy named Marcion, from the Black Sea area, who in the middle of the second century gained a huge following in the Christian community before he was denounced as a heretic in A.D. 144[14] and given this cute nickname by Polycarp: "First-born of Satan."[15] Now I don't want to be judgmental, but I feel like the early church fathers could have seen this one coming. How did this conversation go, exactly? A pasty guy cloaked all in black shows up to the local elders meeting and says, "Hello, I have some great ideas about theology."

"Oh? What's your name?"

"Marcion of the Black Sea!"

"Do you have a nickname, maybe?"

"Yes, First-born of Satan."

"Okay, sounds great! No background check necessary!"

Did not even *one* church father say, "Hey, is it just me or does this guy sound like literally every Disney villain ever?"

Hindsight is twenty-twenty, I guess, and Marcion was allowed to have a big following for quite a while. Marcion taught that the Old Testament was at odds with true Christianity. He thought all the talk about justice and mercy and procreation and helping the poor was rude and crass and way too worldly for God. Jesus's goal wasn't to deal with these trite earthly realities. Marcion had a new idea, which he borrowed from the Greek philosopher Plato: Jesus wanted to save our souls so they could go to heaven. That, for him, was the true gospel. But the early church recognized that if Marcion was correct and heaven was our destination, that is, in effect, a denial of the gospel of Jesus.

Here's the early church father Tertullian on Marcion:

> [According to Marcion,] they are saved only so far as the soul is concerned, but lost in their body, which, according to him, does not rise again. . . . [But if] salvation [is] to the soul alone, this were the better life which we now enjoy whole and entire; whereas to rise again but in part will be a chastisement, not a liberation . . . You display Him as a merely good God; but you are unable to prove that He is perfectly good, because you are not by Him perfectly delivered.[16]

Tertullian's argument is that any god who is interested in saving our souls but has no interest in our actual humanity—our bodies, emotions, human culture, injustices—can't be truly good. If that's who God is, our life now is "the better life," because being a soul without a body would be more like hell than heaven—"a chastisement, not a liberation." My man Augustine makes the same criticism: "When some people say that they would rather be without a body altogether, they entirely deceive themselves."[17]

The God of the Bible, they both argue, must be committed to

redeeming *all* our human experience. He *must* be about heaven coming to earth, *not* earth being destroyed for heaven. Only a God who "perfectly delivers" all our humanity—including our bodies and the world we live in—can be called truly loving and truly good. The god of escapist Evangelicalism—Marcion's Gnostic god—is not the same as the God who renews creation. And that is what the Jesus of Scripture has come to do.

> The Spirit of the Lord is on me,
>   because he has anointed me
>   to proclaim good news to the poor.
> He has sent me to proclaim freedom for the prisoners
>   and recovery of sight for the blind,
> to set the oppressed free,
>   to proclaim the year of the Lord's favor. (Luke 4:18–19)

We see the word *gospel* here ("good news"), but where is *heaven*? The answer is this: It's coming. Here. To earth. The rest of Jesus's ministry speaks likewise. The kingdom isn't going to shrink and die until the world finally burns in a great tribulation. Rather, Jesus says the kingdom of God is like a seed, entrenched in the earth, that grows and fills everything (Luke 13:18–19). The church is like salt, preserving what's good in the world, and light, revealing what's true in order to restore what's beautiful (Matthew 5:13; Luke 8:16–17). The world is like a woman in birth pangs, waiting for the kingdom of God to emerge (Matthew 24:8; see also Romans 8:19–22). The world is like a set of coins that we must take responsibility for or face the consequences when our Master *returns* (Luke 19:11–27). This is why Mark—and the other gospel writers—summarized Jesus's entire gospel message this way: "Jesus went into Galilee, proclaiming the good news [gospel] of God. 'The time has come,' he said. 'The kingdom of God has come near. Repent and believe the good news [gospel]!'" (Mark 1:14–15).

Even Jesus's name implies the gospel is about heaven crashing to earth. Christ means "anointed." This title is special, because it refers to an ancient Jewish ceremony where a leader—a prophet, priest, or king—was bathed in expensive oil, starting with their head and dripping all the way down to their toes. Oil, in the Old and New Testament, is a symbol of healing. To pour oil is to say, "This is where the healing touch of heaven kisses earth." To be anointed meant that you were participating in God's restoration of the world. That's who Messiah is. He is the one who will bring the "healing of the nations" (Revelation 22:2). This is why the Bible includes so many *re-* words. Restoration. Redemption. Rewards. Repentance. Resurrection. *Re-* words mean "we're not starting over somewhere else; we're restoring things to the way they should be." Here. Now. Forever.

Sadly, most evangelicals are walking about with some form of the Gnostic/Marcionite story in our heads. Escape, we are told, is the Christian dream. We even hear the word *resurrection* and think, *Oh, you mean going to heaven!* even though that's the *opposite* of what Jesus's resurrection means. It's not our fault. Those poor students on the quad that day? They'd been taught Marcionism. They thought Jesus was going to vacuum-suction them out of earth. And Michael? He'd been taught a version of the same—the idea that "Your earthly life doesn't matter." I've argued that evangelicals' story about life tends to be about *exclusion* or *relevance*. But these cynical narratives come from a larger narrative, or what is sometimes called a "metanarrative." And that larger, cynical metanarrative for evangelicals in the past several decades is the story of *escape*.

I consider students like Michael to be heroes. They've

grown up in the faith. They believe that Jesus is the Son of God. But the God-breathed image bearer in them won't get on board with the narrative of escape. There is something *good* deep in their bodies and souls that resists this story. As we'll explore next, the story of escape is in many ways the opposite of the story Jesus is telling. Jesus's story is about restoring love, beauty, and freedom to the world. It's a story that frees us to dream again. It's time for us to be re-storied.

7

Re-storied

Cynicism is easy. It doesn't take effort to see what's wrong
with everything and everyone and let it jade us. Hope,
however, is difficult. Maybe because it's heavenly.
　　　　　—JACKIE HILL PERRY, *Upon Waking*

Moreover, in the Catholic Church itself, all possible care
must be taken, that we hold that faith which has been believed everywhere, always, by all.
　　　　　—SAINT VINCENT OF LERINS, *Commonitorium*

Five years ago, I started waking up in a cold sweat, and I
was thinking about dying. You can think about death in an
abstract way, the way you think about economics or the postal
service or where Jell-O comes from, but this wasn't that. I
was thinking about my own personal death. How would it
feel to *die*? Dying is a once-in-a-lifetime event. So to speak.
No one can prepare you for it. I imagined my heart slowing
down. Would I know death was upon me? *Oh no, here it
comes. It's happening.* Or would death mug me like a bum in
an alley? *What if I panic? That would be embarrassing since
I'm supposed to be telling people how to be confident in the
face of death.*

"Some pastor he was, dying in a panic like that!" people
would say as they shook their heads at my grave. "What a

joke! I don't believe in Jesus anymore." For a while, I thought it was a good idea to come up with a great final joke just for my deathbed. Oscar Wilde did that. A few weeks before he died, he said, "My wallpaper and I are fighting a duel to the death. One or the other of us has to go."[1] I love that joke. Maybe I could say my joke, wink, and then *whoosh.* Gone. Never to be seen again . . . alive. But it would be a risk, because if the joke didn't land, well, that was that. Besides, in the end, a final joke is probably too macabre for a pastor. And a Jesus joke would be just terrible.

So here is what I decided is the most likely thing to happen: I will probably spend my last few hours thinking about the wonderful opportunities I had in life and how I basically squandered every single one of them. I'll think about how my wife, Brenna, didn't deserve a schmuck like me. I'll think about what a terrible and emotionally unengaged father I was, and probably still am, lying there on my deathbed. I'll probably think about all the clippings lying around my office from half-baked ideas and unfinished projects I thought I'd complete one day but didn't.

Well, it's too late now, I'll probably think. Then the heart monitor will flatline.

Why did I start thinking about death like this? I have no idea, but I think it had something to do with watching biographical films and documentaries, because I realized in watching those films that life is nothing like them. In the movies, your life has a beginning, middle, and end, like a great story. But in real life, you have a beginning and a middle, but the end is just kind of *whenever.* One person's lifetime isn't like a movie at all. It's more like a random clip from a movie, where we're all left wondering what the point of it was. In that way, life is like a half-finished sen—

The end.

Like that.

All this made me think of the ghost of Jacob Marley in Charles Dickens's *A Christmas Carol,* who looked the scrupulous old miser Ebenezer dead in the eyes as Scrooge fumbled about with half apologies for his greed. Marley said, "No space of regret can make amends for one life's opportunity misused."[2]

Ouch.

I don't know how you feel about ghosts, but that one did a good job summarizing what I was feeling about my life.

This really morbid phase lasted for over a year, and I didn't tell anyone about it. But one night I was in a hotel room with my friend Justin at a ministry conference, and I saw a little ugly green book on his desk.* Justin has good taste. He likes to take old songs by dead people that sound like funeral dirges and put the lyrics to upbeat bluegrass tunes, which is a beautiful hobby and the kind of thing that makes me think, *You are just weird enough to be trusted.* So I picked up the little booger-green book, which was about the Old Testament book Ecclesiastes, and flipped through the pages. I stayed up all night reading it. Ecclesiastes is dark and broody. It talks about death. It talks about how pointless life can feel and probably most likely is. It says strange things: Life is a vapor. It's short. It's hard. It's beautiful. Stop trying to outrun death. You can't out-achieve it. You can't distract yourself from it. Stop living like you're not going to die. You will. Now live your life in light of that.[3]

---

* I actually have a thing for ugly little green books. I hope the book you're holding doesn't look that way, but it's amazing the number of hideously designed pea or booger-green books I've collected, and they are all somehow just lovely inside, once you get to know them. It is probably an irrational theory, but I think that there's something to this correlation and that somebody should do their PhD dissertation on it.

I was surprised to see the Bible naming these things. I wish I had known earlier. Maybe someday I will write a children's book about Ecclesiastes so people will know. It could be for reading aloud at school assemblies or for kindergarten graduation ceremonies, and it could say,

Once upon a time you were born,
But we always knew you were going to die.
So stop trying to cheat death
By leaving a legacy that death will wipe away
Or by distracting yourself with video games,
Because sooner or later you'll realize,
    Death comes to us all.

The only thing is, I will have a hard time finding an illustrator.

A SUPREMELY WEIRD BOOK

This experience with the sickly green book was important for me, because it showed me the Bible was a strange book, which to me meant the Scriptures had some credibility. Somehow—between Worldview camp and sermons that presented the Bible like it was one long book of three-point messages for living or a guidebook for being a White American—I'd grown to distrust the Bible, because I tend to distrust things that tell us "This is the way to be normal or act normal or believe normal."

But this experience with Ecclesiastes was not like that at all. The book of Ecclesiastes is basically God saying, "You know, if I had your perspective, I'd be depressed too." It was incredibly generous of God to say that. In that way, Ecclesiastes affirmed me. It named my experience, and it didn't pull punches. That's what I mean when I say something is just weird enough to be trusted. Weird things are honest things. Normal people are just weird people in hiding. But the Bible is *supremely* weird, come to find out. Ecclesiastes went on to talk about how friends can make life a little better, how it's important to find a job you really like, and how simple things like stopping to enjoy meals can make a big difference.

This is great! I thought.

But the book of Ecclesiastes didn't stop there. In the very last chapter, the author invited us to expand our imaginations and think about life from God's perspective: "Fear God and keep his commandments. . . . For God will bring every deed into judgment" (12:13–14). Even though Ecclesiastes *affirmed* and *named* my experience and said, "Yes, life can feel depressing and pointless 'under the sun' (or from our perspective)," it also invited me to consider that God has a perspective, too, and from His perspective, it's important to care for the poor and the immigrant and the fatherless and the widow. And God will judge everyone for how they do this (or don't). So in the end, the message of Ecclesiastes is something like this: "Enjoy your life, but also keep in mind that God is going to judge everything you do, which is actually good news, because it means life isn't a meaningless cycle of repetition, even though it definitely feels that way *for sure.* So just try to have fun, but don't be a jerk to orphans, because of divine judgment. Good luck with that. The end."

What a quirky little book. I loved it.

I tell you all this because perhaps this is actually the way the Bible is supposed to work on us. On the one hand, it helps us name the janky experiences we're having in life. That may be surprising to you, like it was to me. But I think that's because evangelicals have tried so hard to tame the Bible into something "normal." Something like us. So we gloss over its accounts of petty rivalries, sexual tensions, dark thoughts, and unblinking character studies. And if that's the way you've experienced the Bible, I understand why it feels like a suspicious book. You've experienced people using it as an *excluding* document. For a long time, I thought evangelicals were bibliolaters, having a high reverence for the Bible. When I saw the way they were using it as a weapon against certain kinds of people, it made me think the Bible was the problem. What is actually true is that evangelicals misuse Scripture, demonstrating a low reverence for it, because they are culturologists. They often treat the Bible like a document teaching people how to be *more like us,* which is a bit funny, considering it was written for ancient, emancipated Middle Eastern Jewish nomads. It is not at all like a series of essays about cleaning life up to look "normal." If it were that, I would crumple it up and throw it in the garbage.

But now it is impossible for me to read the Bible like that.

The truth is, the Bible includes all of life's quirks and dark corridors because it is realistic. It is just weird enough to be trusted. It names the human experience in ways unlike any other document I've read. Ecclesiastes did that for me. If Scripture has some divine element to it, we should anticipate it doing more work than could be done by a Tik-Tok self-love guru. It's a book that should stretch us into—as the modern prophetess Billie Eilish once put it—"something I'm not, but something I can be. Something I wait for. Something I'm made for."[4]

The book of Ecclesiastes reminded me God has a perspective on life, too, and because of that, it invited me to get out of my own head, which can be really refreshing. The author put my teeny little life in context: No, by itself, life doesn't have any lasting meaning. But if God is eternal, life can actually be filled with joy and meaning. And because of that, you'd better live like life is meaningful, you can celebrate work and food and drink, and also, don't treat your friends and family and immigrants like garbage. God cares about those people, and He's going to judge you for the way you treat them.

So get a grip, dude. (Translation mine.)

I know it sounds strange, but this reality check helped me start sleeping at night. As it turns out, I needed Ecclesiastes to affirm what I had been feeling. But I also needed it to help me *reimagine* my anxiety, and *integrate* it into the beautiful story Jesus is telling. I desperately needed both, not just one or the other. If the Bible had excluded my experience of fear of death by saying, "You should stop doing that. You think too much," I would have been sadder and more depressed. If it only named my experience and said, "You do you, man, you gothic weirdo. Keep being freaked out, you wonderful freaky man," I would have been sadder and more depressed. But Ecclesiastes did both.

It helped me name my experience *and* reimagine it.

It was the re-storying I needed to be restored.

BIBLIOLATRY

A young friend of mine—we'll call him Samuel—told me he was deconstructing his faith. He said for him, the process was like redecorating a room he'd lived in his whole life. He was taking down the old musty antiques and the fading wallpaper, replacing them with things he really liked, such as jars of pistachios and wacky wallpaper with little flamingos and some shrubs and maybe tiny squirrels hiding in the bushes.

"That sounds like a great little apartment," I responded. "I'd like to go there!" I said that because Samuel is a beautiful, quirky person who listens to offbeat podcasts about topics like how teddy bears are made and what comedians do at pool parties and how any homegrown, small-town friendship could end in murder.

Just weird enough to be trusted.

"Thanks!" Samuel said.

"But I'm also wondering," I continued, "what makes this little apartment *Christian*. If you don't mind me asking."

"What do you mean? It's Christian because it's about Jesus."

"Yeah," I said. "But is it, though?"

"Of course it is," Samuel answered. He leaned way back and folded his arms, which people tell me is something I should pay more attention to, because it means someone thinks maybe I'm being too aggressive and they're worried I might scratch them on the chin or flick straw-wrapper wads at their nose.

That's what they worry about, but I would *never* do that.

So I tried to say something nice.

"Oh," I replied. "Well, your room sounds great. I can see you doing really well in it."

"You do realize it's a metaphor, right?"

"Of course! It's a metaphor about you being you. You're saying Christianity has space for you. It's not some cultural mold you need to fit in. The Bible brings *out* your beauty and the beauty of other cultures. It doesn't squash them . . . even if the evangelical church does. Is it something like that?"

Samuel unfolded his arms.

"And I agree with that. I really do," I said. "Christianity wasn't meant to be a little cultural bubble. It has all the space in the world for people to be their quirky little selves. More than any other religion, actually."

"Uh, not the way I've seen it, it doesn't. Evangelicals seem to think anyone who isn't like them isn't really Christian. I'm not about that."

"I've seen that too. But let's think about other religions for a minute. Buddhists and atheists and Hindus and Muslims have all pretty much stayed put where they began. Hinduism is still overwhelmingly Indian. Buddhism is still mostly Asian. Islam is mostly Middle Eastern. Atheism is mostly Western. They've all traveled a little outside their region, but not much. Christianity is the one religion that's traveled into every culture and adapted itself. How?"

"I guess because following Jesus doesn't demand you be one type of culture?"

"Exactly. Christianity has high standards. But it gives breathing room. So we find more Christians in Africa and South America and Asia today than in America by a long shot.[5] That never could have happened if Christianity—true Christianity—demanded people become American or Western. As African scholar Lamin Sanneh once put it, 'Christianity helped Africans become renewed *Africans,* not re-made Europeans.' "[6]

Samuel nodded.

"So like I said, I like your room metaphor. Christianity lets you decorate things the way you want. It honors personalities and cultures. But Christianity also does something else. It *talks back* to us."

"What do you mean it talks back to us?"

"Well, let's think about Jesus," I answered. "On the one hand, Jesus upset the religious leaders because of His radical inclusivity. A great example of this was His conversation with the non-Jewish woman with a racy past in John 4. Jesus offered Himself to her, freely. He didn't demand she become Jewish. He promised her He was creating a movement where she could worship Him as a non-Jew. As a woman. As *herself.* She was thrilled by this news and immediately went home to invite her non-Jewish friends to meet Jesus."

"That's awesome."

"It *is* awesome. And that's where your room decorating metaphor is totally right. Jesus let the woman decorate the room how she wanted . . . which was extremely upsetting to the religious leaders."

"Enough to get Him crucified."

"Exactly. But Jesus doesn't *just* name and affirm cultural beauty. He also *talks back* to cultures and individuals. We see this especially in the way He talked back to the Jewish culture surrounding Him. Jesus said to the conservative religious Pharisees, 'You have neglected the more important matters of the law—justice, mercy and faithfulness.'[7] In other words, 'If the Scriptures' heart beats for the poor, the broken, and the oppressed, so should yours.'"

"I like it."

"Me too. Then Jesus turned to the more progressive Sadducees. He said to them, 'You are in error because you do not know the Scriptures or the power of God.'[8] Do you notice what's true in both of those encounters?"

"Jesus is very punk rock?"

I laughed. "*So* punk rock. But notice what Jesus does. He talks back to the cultures and individuals of His day. And how does He do it? Through the *Scriptures.* See, the problem with the conservatives and the progressives of Jesus's time was this: They weren't letting the Scriptures *talk back* to them. They were picking and choosing which parts to obey. That way, Scripture could be gagged from correcting their wrong thinking or exposing their cultural biases or shedding light on their unjust practices. They made the Scriptures in their own image. Something that looked and sounded more like them."

"That's my whole problem with evangelicals, though. They say they believe the Bible, but they pick and choose what they want to believe in it. They make it seem like the Bible is all about being a White Republican."

"Okay. Sure . . . but what about you?"

"What do you mean what about me? I care about the poor and voiceless. That's why I left Evangelicalism."

"*Have* you left Evangelicalism, though? I'm not so sure. How has Scripture talked back to you recently? How has it corrected your wrong thinking? How has it corrected your cultural biases? How has it exposed *your* behaviors that don't lead to flourishing? Because, I'll be honest, the idea that all of Christianity is your own personal room? That sounds like the most evangelical thing I've ever heard. 'Here's Christianity. Have it *my* way.'"

My friend laughed a little. "I guess I can see that."

"Look," I said, "I don't blame you for thinking that way. But if you want to get away from evangelical culture, you've got to get away from the evangelical framework. So let me add a couple of contours to your metaphor, okay?"

Samuel nodded but looked skeptical.

"That room of yours needs a foundation. Decorate it however you want, but it needs a blueprint, or it'll crumble. That's why Jesus compared religion not founded on His words to building sandcastles on the beach. When hard times come, it'll be washed away. So what did Jesus say are the *foundations* of faith? The Scriptures. Citing a slight grammatical point about the use of a plural noun in Psalms, Jesus reinforced His point by stating what was well understood by every faithful Hebrew: 'Scripture cannot be broken.'[9] That's because it's written 'by the Spirit.'[10] God Himself. So, like the foundation of a house, they can't be changed or adjusted. 'Not the smallest letter, not the least stroke of a pen, will by any means disappear.'[11] Jesus never talked about rabbinic writings or other teachers that way. That's language a Jewish man would only reserve for God's own words. The Scriptures are the spaces where God *talks back* to us. Otherwise, the thing we're calling Christianity is just an echo chamber for our own opinions and biases."

I could tell Samuel was feeling a little triggered by the conversation. I told him to go ahead and tell me what he was thinking.

"I've seen evangelicals use the Bible to exclude people," said Samuel. "And they call everything they do 'biblical.' I'm just so sick of it all. Being honest, why should I trust your 'biblical' over their 'biblical'?"

I thought for a moment and fiddled with my little balled-up straw wrappers. "I get that, Samuel. I really do. But before I answer, let's think beyond our own experiences to the history of our country. We both know of the Christians who used the Bible to justify slavery. But how did the Black community rise up against all this oppression? By using the Scriptures to talk back to American greed and racism. In fact, early evangelicals were at the forefront of this movement. The Scriptures formed the music, the sermons, and the moral vision for abolition. Later, it did the same for the civil rights movement."

"That doesn't sound like the evangelical church I know."

"Sure. We took a wrong turn, and that's a long story. But the long and short of it is this: Around the late nineteenth century, evangelicals started making some interesting choices about how we *interpret* the Bible. But what those choices *actually* did was isolate us from the global, historic church. And here's where, if I can, I'd like to expand your metaphor even further."

"Oh, great." Samuel rolled his eyes, but he laughed. "Go ahead."

"Okay," I said. "Let's think a little more about the way Jesus described following Him. Did He describe it like being in a room alone, putting up curtains? Because that doesn't sound like the life of a Christian. That just sounds like you're

Batman, and I'm pretty sure he is not a Christian. Also, you should see the Lego version of Batman because it makes this very clear. I think Jesus has something better. Here's the way He described our faith: 'Everyone who has left houses or brothers or sisters or father or mother or wife or children or fields for my sake will receive a *hundred* times as much and will inherit eternal life.'[12] Hundreds of houses and people. What does that sound like?"

"Like . . . a city?"

"Exactly. Not just a room. A city. Or a village, which sounds more quaint and friendly, like the one from *Beauty and the Beast,* with a little library and singing birds."

"You know," my friend said, "if the Spanish Inquisition had tortured metaphors, you could have had a great career as a priest."

I laughed. "Thank you? Look. Here's my point. In order to let the Scriptures talk back to us, we need to let the global, historic village of the church *help us* apply them. Otherwise, we'll just skip past the parts we don't like. So we need to read them through the eyes of martyrs; through church councils who dove deep into the Scriptures, collaborated, and argued out the nuances; through brilliant pastors and theologians over the centuries who've taken wrong turns and said, 'This is a dead end. Don't go that route.' We need the Christian village, filled with faithful Jesus followers all around the globe. Africans and Asians and even Canadians."

"Even Canadians?"

"Yes, *even Canadians*. Actually, I'll get back to you on the Canadian thing. The point is, Christianity isn't just a room. It's a village. So here's what I would say to you and to the Evangelicalism you're deconstructing: Step outside. Christianity's a lot bigger than us. The air is great. You don't need to be cooped up in a room alone. Christianity is an ancient, beautiful, global village. You can be part of it."

"Okay," he replied. "I get what you're saying."

He took another long pause, and I put my little straw wrappers in my pocket.

"Here's the thing," he said. "I'm tired. I've seen so much pain and abuse in the church. The idea of 'reconstructing' my faith feels overwhelming."

"I 100 percent agree with you. That's why I'm not asking you to reconstruct your faith. I'm asking you to let the global, historic church renew you and restore you. To give you a new story to live from. What you've been living in is the world of American Evangelicalism. I'd like to invite you back to historic Protestantism."

"But that's the thing. Where would I even start?"

"Here's what I would do. Start by asking, 'What is the gospel story the global, historic Christian village has been telling for two thousand years?' Because I think it's actually *very* different from the evangelical story—the story of escape—that we American evangelicals have been telling for a century now. In some ways, it's an *opposite* story."

"Okay," he said. "And where do we find this 'opposite story'?"

"I'd start with a guy the global church has looked to for daily gospel guidance for a few centuries now."

"Who? Martin Luther?"

"Nope. I'm thinking of someone who proclaims the gospel as one big, beautiful story. A story I'll bet you've never heard. And I think that's what you need, really. Not some reconstruction project. No. What you need is to feel renewed. *Restored. Re-storied.* And I have just the man for the job."

"Of course it's a man. Probably a White man, right?"

"Yes, a man. Definitely not White. But he *did* write this gospel summary while he was being humiliated for not being like his obedient and faithful wife, Elizabeth."

"Okay, I'll bite. Who is it?"

"The New Testament prophet Zechariah."

"I've literally never heard anyone talk about Zechariah."

"That's because you've been living in the White evangelical house for too long, my friend. The global, historic church has been singing Zechariah's song every day for a few centuries now. They've done it through a book South Americans, Europeans, Roman Catholics, Africans, and even a spare few Americans use to pray daily: the Book of Common Prayer. Zechariah's prayer—called the Benedictus—is the first thing these Christians pray in the morning . . . But it doesn't gel too well with the gospel that American evangelicals proclaim, so I'm not surprised you haven't heard much about it. Could I let Zechariah show us around the village?"

"If you say so," said my friend. "But I am literally never going to use a metaphor within one hundred feet of you again."

"Would you be surprised to hear I've heard that before?"

"No. Not really. Not at all."

8

Zechariah

At long last, perhaps there is an empire larger than the Empire that has been devouring us by inches. Perhaps now it comes. Perhaps now I will be able to stop waiting.
　　　　—ARKADY MARTINE, *A Memory Called Empire*

There's something out there far from my home
A longing that I've never known.
　　　　—"JACK'S LAMENT," from *The Nightmare Before Christmas*

To understand Zechariah's prayer, we have to understand his story—intimately and deeply. So if you'd permit me a risk . . . I'd like to imagine it with you. My hope is that you can see that it's a story that names our pain and grief and longings and quirkiness.

Zechariah is . . . complicated. Not perfect. But he's not a bad guy either. He needs to be renewed. Restored. Re-storied. He's a man whose faith has been shattered, but it's not gone. It's been disillusioned by pain, both inside and outside the church. And it's been dimmed by his own unbelief. Yet the story ends with not a neat little bow but a glint in the eye. Zechariah finds the thing he's been looking for all along: a sense of hope.

———

Imagine Zechariah, a priest, and his wife, Elizabeth, celebrating the Passover by candlelight in the dark of their home, the shadows flickering along the walls. Notice the barren quiet of their childless home. They've been praying for five long decades, "Lord, grant us a child."

Silence.

Maybe they stopped praying that prayer a long time ago. By the time we meet them in the book of Luke, Elizabeth is not only infertile but also past the age of childbearing. They would have known the story of Abraham's wife, Sarah, bearing a child in her old age. Then again, Sarah was special. Since her time, countless childless Jewish couples had been forgotten, then scrubbed from the lineage of their forefathers and erased from the annals of history. Zechariah and Elizabeth would be among them. Making matters worse, a childless woman was—in ancient Jewish thought—likely cursed. In the marketplace, no one would say this to them. It was all in the averted gaze. The quickened pace of the feet. Today, as Luke's story begins, we see Zechariah stepping out into the Jerusalem streets. He hears the chorus of children and feels a pang in his chest.

"Lord, forgive me," Zechariah whispers. "Purify my heart. I pray for these little ones, the sons of my brothers . . ." His eyes wander toward imperial guards, huddled around his friend Jacob's fruit stand. One centurion picks at Jacob's figs and almonds, the fruit he's grown with his own hands. The fruit is Rome's by right . . . or so they think. Zechariah can't watch. His wife is barren. So is his nation, Jerusalem. God had cursed them all with Rome's empire. When would they be restored? Ever?

Zechariah would have been born around 63 B.C., the year of Roman occupation. Maybe he felt haunted by the significance of his birth, like an awful birthmark. Maybe it gave him delusions of grandeur. Surely, as a child, he had pictures of

Yahweh raising him up to fight the enemies of Israel, like
Judas Maccabeus had done. But Rome was subtler than the
Seleucids Judas had staved off, who had tried to keep the
Jews under their thumb. Rome had conquered many coun-
tries. They knew how to prevent revolt.

They knew how to *castrate* a nation.

When the Romans occupied, they came proclaiming something they called "the gospel," or the *euangelion*. It was proclaimed, loud and clear, the year Augustus took his father's
throne. An ancient calendar inscription refers to Augustus as
"a savior" and goes on to say, "The birthday of the god Augustus was the beginning of the *good tidings* for the world."

It was a less-than-subtle assault—or so it seemed to the
Jews—on the prophet Isaiah's gospel:

How beautiful on the mountains
    are the feet of those who bring good news,
who proclaim peace,
    who bring good tidings [gospel],
    who proclaim salvation,
who say to Zion,
    "Your God reigns!" (52:7)

For Rome, Caesar Augustus was savior of the world, and the
so-called Jewish Anointed One was only one of his many subjects. Caesar would bring the peace of Rome (the Pax Romana)
to the world, not the peace of God—*shalom*. The Romans
happily condescended to the Jews, so long as functionally—
in reality—*Caesar* was lord. This is why Rome let the He-
brews have their customs, celebrate their feasts, worship their
God. Rome's mock gospel was built on Jewish backs.

I imagine little Zechariah having a conversation with his
father, who would have also been a priest.

"Look at our people," his father would say to Zechariah,

watching the Romans' limestone, technology, and blood money go into the rebuilding of the Jewish temple. "Are we back in Egypt? Are we slaves of the Romans?"

"But this is *our* temple, Father," replies young Zechariah. "Rabbi Simon says that when the temple is rebuilt, Messiah will come." Zechariah's father is silent.

Finally, he asks, "If a man divorces his wife and sends her away, then sends her flowers, what do the flowers mean to her?"

"Nothing, Father," says Zechariah. "But the man did not make the flowers. Yahweh did."

Zechariah's father looks down at him, as though seeing him for the first time. He laughs. "You are beginning to speak like a priest," he says.

"Thank you," responds Zechariah.

"I never said it was a good thing!" He sweeps Zechariah up in his arms, buffs his forehead, then kisses it. "You will be an excellent priest, my son," he says, winking. "Just like your father. And so will your sons and their sons . . ."

———

We follow Zechariah, now an old man, along the streets, past Jacob's fruit stand and toward the temple. Smell the roasted goat with garlic, baked sweet raisin bread, and sour wine. Luke's story takes place on the Day of Atonement, an annual pilgrimage for Jewish worshippers everywhere to the Jerusalem temple for a sacrificial ritual. Zechariah watches the money changers at the temple gates, exchanging currencies.

A woman with her two sons inquires about the price of a pigeon. When she hears the price, her face falls. "That is twice as much as last year," she pleads.

The merchant shrugs. "The Roman pigs take half of my earnings," he replies.

"I will pay for the woman's honorable sacrifice. I would rather *give* blood money than take it," Zechariah says quietly, fixing his gaze on the merchant.

In the temple courts, thousands of priests like Zechariah are gathered in the Court of Priests. Like most of them, Zechariah has never entered the temple's inner sanctum, where the Shekinah glory of Yahweh dwells. Or at least . . . it had, in the time of David. The inner sanctum is closed by a shining bronze door with gold-plated leaves and flanked by grand white pillars. But even when he sees the arresting beauty of it, he feels nauseous. How could such a beautiful thing— Yahweh's own temple—bring him such a feeling of alienation? Even . . . disgust? Esau had sold his own birthright for a pot of stew.

Yes, that is what this temple is. A large pot of stew. Nothing more.

Now he's whisked away for the casting of lots, an annual ritual for the Day of Atonement.

"Zechariah," asks a fellow priest, "you have never been chosen to enter the holy place?"

Zechariah shakes his head. "It is a once-in-a-lifetime event," he says. "Twenty thousand priests and two offerings a day. That means for most of us . . . perhaps in the next lifetime."

The high priest is standing near the altar now, holding a bundle of reeds, one for each priest. Zechariah approaches, as he's done each morning and evening for decades, never being chosen. He remembers an older priest who had never entered the inner sanctum comparing this process to marrying a woman but never lying with her.

Or never conceiving, Zechariah thinks.

The court falls silent as the high priest draws the chosen reed.

"Zechariah!"

The high priest's voice echoes around the courtyard.

Then . . . cheers. His fellow priests' shouts make his ears ring, but his heart feels dead. He feels hands grip his shoulders, whispers and shouts of congratulations coming at him from every direction.

How can a barren man be chosen to enter Yahweh's presence?

Now he's surrounded by priests, directing him to the washing basin, drenching him in purified water, and rushing him toward the sanctuary. The bowl of spices—onycha, galbanum, frankincense—is placed in his hand. Zechariah chokes a bit on the fragrance. He's trembling. Why? Fear of Yahweh's presence?

Or even worse . . . fear that when he enters, there will be absence? A void. Nothing.

Zechariah's heart pounds. He walks toward the plated gates, into the forbidden sanctuary, and the sight within makes his knees nearly buckle. To his left and right, the menorahs burn their candles, illuminating brilliant, shimmering gold walls. The walls are engraved, as he had been told, with the symbolic echoes of the garden—angels, palm trees, flowers. Before him is the altar of incense and, beyond, the beautiful interwoven curtain of purple, white, and red guarding the holy of holies. But one thing captures Zechariah's eyes as he walks toward the altar of incense: Two cherubim—great, alien messengers of Yahweh—are woven into the curtain. They stand guard, as the cherubim in the garden had done, and look at him.

Zechariah lifts his head to pray for his people—the most important prayer of his life.

Something stops him. A glimmer of light. He looks about. *The small east window, of course.* The sun has risen high enough now that its beams reflect off the cherubim, making them gleam. It's brilliant artwork. Designed, perhaps, for this very moment.

Zechariah laughs at himself.

He turns back to the altar to offer his prayers.

Then he falls back, as though struck.

A light, blinding like nothing he'd ever seen, strikes his eyes. The incense bowl dashes along the golden floor. A voice like thunder fills the sanctuary. Zechariah lays himself flat.

"Do not be afraid, Zechariah," booms the voice. "Your prayer has been heard." Zechariah sees a man standing before him, or what looks like a man, with piercing eyes. His robes are whiter than white. The angel approaches him and gestures for Zechariah to stand.

"Elizabeth, your wife, will bear a son by you. You are to name him John. You will leap like a gazelle for joy, and not only you—many will delight in his birth. He'll achieve great stature with God. He will drink neither wine nor beer. He will be filled with the Holy Spirit while still in his mother's womb. He will turn many sons and daughters of Israel back to their God and will herald God's arrival in the strength of Elijah. He'll soften the hearts of parents to children and kindle devotion among those who doubt."

Now the man pauses and looks long at Zechariah.

He concludes, "He will prepare people for God's arrival."

"And how, exactly . . ." Zechariah searches for words. "How exactly will these things be so? I am an old man. My wife is barren."

The angel's eyes seem to burn. His light grows blinding, and his voice thunderous.

"I am Gabriel, messenger of Yahweh, sent especially to bring you this glad news. But because you won't believe me, you'll be unable to say a word until the day of your son's birth. Every word I've spoken to you will come true in Yahweh's time."

In a blink, the temple is empty.

Zechariah stands. The empty bowl of incense lies at his feet. The curtain stands before him, the two woven cherubim looking on. Inanimate. The crackling of incense returns to Zechariah's ears. He begins to pray the ritual words. No sound comes from his mouth. He tries again. Nothing. Tears flood his eyes.

And then . . . Zechariah laughs.

His laughter is hoarse, barely audible. But it's filled with something he hasn't felt in his bones for a long, long time. Not sadness. Not doubt. Something else. He doesn't know why or how, but something dead has come alive. Something old and dusty and tucked away is breaking forth. In the same way Yahweh had spoken creation into existence—somehow, the angel had brought him back to life. Zechariah suddenly yearns for the presence of Elizabeth. What would she say, now? She would take his hand and thank Yahweh for the gift before him.

Thank You.

No more darkness inside.

No more barrenness.

Light.

THE BENEDICTUS

There is a lot of debate about Zechariah's character. Was he punished for unbelief? Or was he a faithful, "righteous" believer? I think Zechariah was trying to believe. He asked for assurance, because he *wanted* to believe. But something in him couldn't go there anymore. He needed a severe mercy, and that's what was granted to him. The idea of making an old, broken man mute might seem harsh to us. But it's also exactly what he asked for: Zechariah asked for a sign. So, the angel gave one, like a bucket of cold water to a sleeping man. We know this wasn't meant to harm Zechariah, because the angel didn't revoke God's promises to him. No, he did just the opposite. He confronted Zechariah with God's promises— a dare to believe.

Why muteness, then? Because in that silent, creative space, Zechariah found room to dream. In the months of silence, the Spirit *re-storied* Zechariah. He refreshed him with the fantastical, whirring promises of the story he was meant to live in. Zechariah wanted a child and ultimately a legacy, and God would give him those, but it could be said that the Lord found Zechariah's dreams "not too strong, but too weak."[1] Instead of giving Zechariah only an earthly legacy, God placed his good desire for a child into the large, sweeping narrative of the Scriptures. Zechariah's dreams were fulfilled within God's dreams. Without this severe mercy, the Benedictus prayer Zechariah wrote at the birth of his son would never have been crafted.

Zechariah remained mute for months. Enough time to think and compose the prayer we know today as the Benedictus. And here is the result, according to Luke 1:68–79:

Praise be to the Lord, the God of Israel,
    because he has come to his people and redeemed
        them.
He has raised up a horn of salvation for us
    in the house of his servant David
(as he said through his holy prophets of long ago),
salvation from our enemies
    and from the hand of all who hate us—
to show mercy to our ancestors
    and to remember his holy covenant,
    the oath he swore to our father Abraham:

to rescue us from the hand of our enemies,
>and to enable us to serve him without fear
>in holiness and righteousness before him all our
>days.

And you, my child, will be called a prophet of the Most
High;
>for you will go on before the Lord to prepare the
>way for him,
to give his people the knowledge of salvation
>through the forgiveness of their sins,
because of the tender mercy of our God,
>by which the rising sun will come to us from heaven
to shine on those living in darkness
>and in the shadow of death,
to guide our feet into the path of peace.

Look to the wild, free promises Zechariah sang about. He had been re-storied. His vision of God was no longer one of cynicism but one of hope. It's not a story about escape. It's a story that begins with the words "Praise be to the Lord, the God of Israel, because *he has come to [us]*." The gospel, for Zechariah, is something like this: God has arrived.

9

Shalom

He looked at Natasha as she sang, and something new and joyful stirred in his soul. He felt happy and at the same time sad. . . . The chief reason was a sudden, vivid sense of the terrible contrast between something infinitely great and illimitable within him and that limited and material something that he, and even she, was.
—LEO TOLSTOY, *War and Peace*

All these same miseries prove man's greatness. They are the miseries of a great lord, of a deposed king.
—BLAISE PASCAL, *Pensées*

Years ago I learned the German word *Sehnsucht.* It doesn't describe happiness or sadness. It describes a happy sadness. Or a sadness that comes from happiness. A "yearning." An *ache.* It's a feeling of being homesick for a place you've never been. Just this afternoon Brenna and I were talking about our dreams. We both have recurring dreams, it turns out, where we have houses, sometimes along with local marketplaces or whole communities. The houses are the same every time. Mine is along the ocean, and you can walk to a marketplace where people are selling coffee and tea and there are warm yellow walls downstairs and people who know my face upstairs. On the corner is an open two-story bookstore with sliding ladders and a little record shop, and beyond that a long dock and a gazebo where a fishmonger is selling fresh iced clams and lobsters. There is a deep feeling of belonging. I've been there hundreds of times. But I've never really been there. I've never been anywhere like that. It's a place my mind created for me. And so, waking from these dreams evokes this feeling of incredible joy . . . and sadness. *Sehnsucht.* Where are we trying to get to? Where's that place in our dreams? Why do we feel the *Sehnsucht*? What—or where or whom— are we homesick for?

The first time I can remember feeling *Sehnsucht* was in my backyard as a kid. I was surrounded by big Michigan blue spruces that seemed as tall as the Eiffel Tower. Those trees always felt like an invitation to me . . . To what, I don't know. Something about them said, "Come climb us. Come make us your home." So I spent a lot of time letting the trees' sap stick to my hands and their bristles scrape me as I scrambled up. Sometimes a mourning dove would sing a little song above me if I was quiet enough. In the summer, my dad's stereo system would often blare good, Southern rock music and I could hear it muted through the glass door. But I also re- member feeling sad. Delighted, for sure. Yet . . . something was missing. I still felt, as much as I climbed those trees and memorized the mourning dove's song, like I was locked out of nature's room. *Sehnsucht.*

Maybe that's why I've always felt weirdly attracted to going to the zoo. The zoo is such a strange place, because we can all go to pretend there is some kind of harmony between us and the natural world. But it is hard not to think of the bul- letproof glass between me and the silverback gorilla; the kib- ble fed to the giraffes, which is a sad excuse for a wild, lush jungle leaf; or how that lion is probably not glaring at me because he's admiring my cardigan. Nothing makes me hap- pier and sadder than visiting a zoo.

Sehnsucht.

This feeling can sneak up on me out of nowhere these days. I recently felt *Sehnsucht* watching Peter Jackson's eight-hour *Get Back* documentary of the Beatles.[1] The whole movie is about Paul and George and Ringo and John bickering about artistry and direction and pretty much everything under the sun. Really, it's a breakup film. It's about their last days together. It went on and on, and I wasn't sure where the film was going, just like with most Peter Jackson films. But then, in the final hour of the series, seemingly out of nowhere, there emerges a moment of magnificent beauty. The Beatles somehow—in the midst of their breakup—pull off a rooftop concert in the middle of London, where they record excerpts from two of the greatest albums of all time, *Let It Be* and *Abbey Road*. It's only then that we learn *what* we've been watching this entire eight-hour slog: the birth of some of the greatest music of the twentieth century, crafted by the fumbling, directionless hands of a few immature twenty-somethings on the verge of a breakup.

I burst into tears. Why? Why couldn't I just say, "Hey, that's great! Glad it happened!"? Because I felt *Sehnsucht.* In the midst of profound beauty, aching sadness. It was the last time the Beatles would ever record together. The beauty couldn't last. Not in this life.

Probably the most common way I see people expressing their *Sehnsucht* these days is through nostalgia. My students— all born in the 2000s—love to nerd out with me about the 1980s and '90s. Or boy bands from the early 2000s. Nostalgia for these decades is wildly popular in TV shows and movies. Even the mullets are making a comeback. Nostalgia is a brilliant way for us to explain away our *Sehnsucht:* "There was a time when true beauty and community and a sense of purpose existed. Now it's gone, which is why you can't have it anymore."

And look, I *was* born in the '80s, but just barely, and I lived through the '90s, rattail haircut and all. It didn't feel like home. It wasn't the place we're looking for. Says the guy who listens to '80s retro synthwave rock on repeat.

The truth is, we were sad back then too. Definitely not as sad, because we didn't have smartphones, which statistically speaking have caused all kinds of depression and anxiety. But we still needed drugs and sex and rock n' roll to try to fill the void inside us. And none of it worked. None of it felt like home. We still had *Sehnsucht*.

So what *are* we looking for?

PEACE

As I mentioned earlier, for my last two undergraduate semesters, I left the nest of my Christian college to study children's literature at Oxford University. That's where I encountered C. S. Lewis's autobiography, *Surprised by Joy*. The thing he described in this book was *Sehnsucht*. Lewis wasn't much of a Beatles fan. For him, *Sehnsucht* came when he read *The Wind in the Willows* as a kid, when his brother, Warnie, made a little nature set for him, and when he read about Balder of Norse mythology dying and rising again. Even as an atheist, Lewis felt a pull toward the transcendent through these things: *Sehnsucht*. In "The Weight of Glory," he described it briefly:

> We do not want merely to *see* beauty. . . . We want something else which can hardly be put into words—to be united with the beauty we see, to pass into it, to receive it into ourselves, to bathe in it, to become part of it.[2]

Recently, I read a book called *Amphibious Soul* written by the award-winning director of the Netflix documentary *My*

Octopus Teacher, Craig Foster. I read it because I've always thought that if I weren't a Christian, I would try to find a sense of transcendence by being a foodie guy or a nature guy. Even better, I would be a foodie nature guy who travels around the world like Anthony Bourdain and tries everyone's delicious food in exotic settings while getting paid for it. Surely that would give me a feeling of transcendence. This is why I was shocked, years ago, when Bourdain took his own life. It's also why I found Foster's description of his own experience, as a nature guy, sobering. Foster wrote about how we all need to return to a paleolithic lifestyle where we forage for berries and track animals and take cold dives into the ocean so we can really feel alive. That, he argued, will make us the people we're trying to be. And yet, at the beginning of the book, he penned these sobering words:

> As a documentary filmmaker, I made it my mission to seek out the greatest naturalists alive. I met skilled trackers who could read animal behavior in ways that seemed fantastical. I learned about community-based healing practices that gave people a rich, multidimensional view of living and dying. And I was introduced to ancient wisdom about reciprocity that seemed crucial for navigating the future of our species.
>
> During that time I also felt a deep sadness, a yearning. I could not put my finger on the source, but it sometimes seemed as if the more illuminating the subjects of my films, the more my heart ached.[3]

Do you hear the *Sehnsucht*?

In his personal letters, Lewis shared that his friend J.R.R. Tolkien was the first to connect for him the feeling of *Sehnsucht* and Christianity. What if Jesus *is* the reality all these things pointed toward? What if there really *was* a place and a person and an experience of reality that his heart was aching for? How else could he explain the ache?

> Now what Dyson and Tolkien showed me was this: that if I met the idea of sacrifice in a Pagan story I didn't mind it at all: again, that if I met the idea of a god sacrificing himself to himself . . . I liked it very much and was mysteriously moved by it. . . .
>
> Now the story of Christ is simply a true myth: a myth working on us in the same way as the others, but with this tremendous difference that *it really happened.*[4]

Jesus's dreams, Lewis concluded, were what his *Sehnsucht* was crying out for. The true myth every story he'd ever been stirred by pointed toward. This shook me. I'd always thought Christianity was about believing a set of answers so we could pass the test to get into heaven. What did Jesus have to do with *the ache*?

As it turns out, everything.

This is *exactly* what Zechariah's prayer is singing to us:

> You, my child [Zechariah's son, John], will be called a
>   prophet of the Most High;
>   for you will go on before the Lord to prepare the
>   way for him,
> to give his people the knowledge of salvation
>   through the forgiveness of their sins,
> because of the tender mercy of our God,
>   by which the rising sun will come to us from heaven
> to shine on those living in darkness
>   and in the shadow of death,
> to guide our feet into the path of peace. (Luke 1:76–79)

Look at this last phrase with me: "To guide our feet into the path of peace."

Imagine asking a typical evangelical, "Why did Jesus come?"

How many of them do you think would answer this way? "Oh, to guide our feet into the path of peace!"

So what in the world is Zechariah talking about?

Peace, for White Americans, often means, "Everybody leave me alone so I can watch Wes Anderson films in the dark while straight-up eating a stick of deli salami." No? Just me? Okay then.

Well, when we talk about peace, we usually mean the absence of something, typically conflict. Noise. Interruptions. But Zechariah isn't merely talking about the absence of conflict. He's talking about something far different: the presence of something remarkably transcendent.

When I was a teenager, I had an older friend Mark who was an incredible electric guitarist. Mark was so good at guitar I felt like I didn't even play the same instrument. When he described the technical specs and mods of his guitar to me, I said, "Yes, those are really nice specs, the best, Mark," but I never knew what he was saying. Sometimes he would ask me about the specs and mods of my guitar, and I would say, "Well, my guitar is red, with some white parts. It also has six strings that I use for strumming." He would laugh because he thought I was joking. One day, Mark and I met up for a jam session, and he said, "Nick, I just scored some Gary Hoey tickets for us." I didn't know who Gary Hoey was, but I didn't want to disappoint Mark, so I did a fist pump and shouted, "Yes!" Two weeks later, I was at a small concert venue of mostly old people. Gary walked onto the stage. He looked like someone who was popular in high school and like maybe he hadn't showered since then. Then Gary Hoey picked up his guitar.

He started with a single, screaming note. He played a little bit with his amplifier until the note sounded just like he wanted. He paused, and my friend Mark winked at me. Then magic happened. Gary's fingers began to dance and shred effortlessly up and down the fretboard. His guitar was making sounds I didn't know guitars could make. At one point I turned to Mark and said, "I wish I had that kind of freedom." I meant about playing the guitar, not about the showering. After a bit, the drummer crashed a cymbal, the bassist boomed, and they were off to the races. Throughout the concert, Mark and I kept looking at each other and laughing. It was like a big, beautiful ghost had entered the room. Something beyond Gary Hoey had entered into the mix, and with it came a transcendent beauty.

Maybe you've felt this kind of harmony while waving a light under the stars at a concert. Or at the climax of a beautiful film. Or while carving wood or playing basketball or knitting, when your body and mind feel—just for a moment—like they're working as one. Or during Christmas dinner with family. These are moments that transcend. When everything or everyone is working as one, it feels as though a third thing has entered the room: the presence of beauty. These experiences are much more like what the Hebrew writers mean when they say, "Shalom." That's because shalom, in the Hebrew mind, is about the *transcendent harmony of everything.* Ourselves and others, the earth, and within. But most of all, shalom is about God's divine presence, running through everything. It's the world in harmony with the divine. Finally restored. It's what our *Sehnsucht* is crying out for.

And that, sings Zechariah, is what Jesus came to bring: transcendent harmony to the earth.

I've written many things to you in this book, reader, but I've not made many claims about *your* life. I'm going to do that now, and I'd do that only if I believed it 110 percent. I wish someone had said this directly to me twenty years ago: Shalom is the thing you've been looking for your entire life.

ANCIENT GOSPEL

In my junior year of college, I discovered an old book by an African man named Augustine, which I was told was the first autobiography ever written. If you want to read something entertaining that also sounds impressive to your book club friends, you should pick it up. It's called *Confessions.* In it, Augustine talks about everything from the philosophy of time to sex dreams, which is pretty saucy stuff for the fourth century. But some of the most interesting things to me in this book were the little glimpses of the church in the fourth century and their version of the gospel.

At the beginning of the book, Augustine shares the story of his conversion. He tells of visiting a little church in Rome, where he heard a man named Ambrose preaching. Augustine had heard that Ambrose was a gifted speaker, and since Augustine was a reputable agnostic professor of rhetoric in Rome, he decided to give him a listen. Augustine went once. Then he went again. And again. Something about Ambrose drew him back, even though he was totally confused by Ambrose's sermons. One day, Augustine got up the gumption to ask Ambrose a question.

"I would like to explore these ideas," Augustine said. "I want to know more about this gospel you are talking about." Now if Ambrose had been an American evangelical, he might have had Augustine kneel down and pray a prayer of acceptance, since, after all, Augustine had been in church *three years* and really should have already done this by now. He might have drawn a little picture on a napkin of Jesus bridging the gap between Augustine and God. He might have told Augustine that God had a wonderful plan for his life and that, through Jesus, all young Augustine's dreams of personal wealth and academic achievement would come true if he just had the power of faith—and oh, by the way, the DVD set of *The Best of Ambrose* was in the back, available for purchase. But he didn't do any of those things. Instead, he said, "You want to understand the gospel? Go read the book of Isaiah."[5]

Ambrose's charge is literally the last thing any of us evangelicals would say to people exploring Christianity. In fact, it might not even crack the top 999. Isaiah is confounding, violent, and filled with obscure visions and strange, sensuous promises about food and wine and national prestige and Lord knows what. Sure, there are the helpful bits about the Virgin Birth and being healed by Jesus's stripes. But we really have to dig for those little gems. The rest, to my evangelical ears, had always felt completely irrelevant.

I wondered, when I first read this story about Saint Augustine, whether this was just an Ambrose thing. But as I investigated early church history, I found that this book—which most evangelicals find obscure and baffling—was commonly seen as central for understanding the gospel. The early church father Jerome wrote, "[Isaiah] should be called an evangelist rather than a prophet, because he describes all the mysteries of Christ and the church so clearly."[6] The book was so honored in the early church, in fact, that Isaiah was commonly referred to as "the fifth gospel," and Isaiah himself was known as "the great prophet." These are not words the evangelicals generally use to describe Isaiah. But Isaiah's ghost haunts the American evangelical church, because the little phrase *good news* or *gospel*—the phrase we all agree summarizes the message of Jesus—comes from the book of Isaiah.

And when Isaiah described *good news,* it sounded *nothing*

like the story of escape we've been telling. Here is how Isaiah 52:7 announces the gospel:

How beautiful on the mountains
    are the feet of those who bring good news [gospel],
who proclaim *peace,*
    who bring good tidings,
    who proclaim salvation,
who say to Zion,
    "Your God reigns!"

For Isaiah, the good news of the gospel is "Your God reigns!" This is why Mark summarized Jesus's entire message this way: "Jesus went into Galilee, proclaiming the good news [gospel] of God. 'The time has come,' he said. 'The kingdom of God has come near. Repent and believe the good news [gospel]!'" (1:14–15).

The reign of God has arrived, and the result is peace. Shalom.

Isaiah wrote of the coming Messiah,

To us a child is born,
    to us a son is given,
    and the government will be on his shoulders.
And he will be called
    Wonderful Counselor, Mighty God,
    Everlasting Father, Prince of Peace [shalom]. (9:6)

The Messiah will bring shalom—transcendent harmony—to all things. That's Isaiah's gospel. This was why Isaiah pictured Messiah's arrival as the natural world bubbling with joy: mountains bursting into song, trees clapping their hands, thornbushes being overgrown by junipers (55:12–13). It's an alienated world made right again, because the divine is re-united, in love, to us. Shalom. And so the heavenly messengers announcing Jesus's birth said,

Glory to God in the highest heaven,
    and on earth *peace* to those on whom his favor
        rests. (Luke 2:14)

The arrival of Jesus means God's kingdom of peace is here at last.

This is also why Paul later described Jesus's message as "the gospel of peace" (Ephesians 6:15) and His ministry as "the ministry of reconciliation" (2 Corinthians 5:18). In fact, Paul went out of his way to show that the gospel means Christ's work is to *make peace* with everyone and everything, both in heaven and on earth:

The Son is the image of the invisible God, the firstborn over all creation. For in him all things were created: things in heaven and on earth, visible and invisible, whether thrones or powers or rulers or authorities; all things have been created through him and for him. He is before all things, and in him all things hold together. And he is the head of the body, the church; he is the beginning and the firstborn from among the dead, so that in everything he might have the supremacy. For God was pleased to have all his fullness dwell in him, and through him to reconcile to himself all things, whether things on earth or things in heaven, by making peace through his blood, shed on the cross. (Colossians 1:15–20)

Jesus's mission wasn't to help us escape earth. Paul said six times in this short passage that Christ made peace with "all things." That includes every part of creation. Heaven and earth, reconciled to God through Christ. Not escape. *Restoration.* Shalom, simply put, is heaven and earth reunited.

It's a world filled with the divine.

It's the world we're all longing for, deep down.

THE SONG OF NEW CREATION

My friend Ben tells me I should stop quoting J.R.R. Tolkien's *Lord of the Rings,* because it's not cool anymore and it makes me sound nerdy, plus no one gets my obscure references. Oh, really, Ben? Then I suppose you thought it was "cool" when Melkor corrupted Fëanorr to betray his half-brother Fingolfin, who was trying to usurp his rightful claim to the throne of the Noldor and steal the Silmarils, even though Fingolfin already CLEARLY pledged his fealty to him? Yeah, SO COOL. Some judge of cool you are, Ben. This illustration's for you.

One reason *The Lord of the Rings* is so beautiful is because of Tolkien's Christian (he was a devout Roman Catholic) vision of what it means to live in a world of shalom. If you are not that into elves and dwarves, just keep in mind that, for Tolkien, these are only symbols of what the world is really like—a world aching for shalom. We see this most explicitly in Tolkien's prequel to *The Lord of the Rings, The Silmarillion,* which, clearly, is deeply indebted to the book of Genesis.

In it, he tells the story of a godlike figure he calls Ilúvatar.

Ilúvatar is a divine being who sings into existence all of creation. Then he gives to everyone something he calls "secret fire," which are men's different gifts and abilities. Once everything is created, the world sings a song of transcendent harmony, conducted by Ilúvatar himself. But some of the creatures decided to sing their own solos, which Tolkien described as—and here I think it's funny to picture Tolkien writing in the room next to his son Christopher, who is rocking to the latest Black Sabbath vinyl—"loud, and vain, and endlessly repeated; and it had little harmony, but rather a clamorous unison as of many trumpets braying upon a few notes."[7] Ilúvatar's world became a world of chaos. Rather than living into Ilúvatar's song, they each decided to make a song about themselves. And that created chaos. That's how we lost shalom.

This, for Tolkien, is the state of the world today: All of us are trying to sing our own solos rather than lean into God's beautiful, harmonious song of shalom. Tolkien said that ever since we humans came "out of tune," we've been listening carefully to the world, trying to hear that original music.

"Yet," he wrote, "we know not for what we listen."

The ache. *Sehnsucht.*

But what comes next points to Tolkien's profound understanding of the gospel of shalom. In response to the rebellion, Ilúvatar made a promise. One day he would resolve the discordance of the world with a beautiful chord that would be "deeper than the Abyss, higher than the Firmament, piercing as the light of the eye of Ilúvatar."[8] He would return the world to transcendent harmony again. Ilúvatar, rather than simply drowning everyone out, which 100 percent would have been my strategy, decided like a great jazz musician to take the dissonance we've made and incorporate it into one final song: Shalom will return. And it will be more beautiful than ever.

What was Tolkien getting at here? What is this final, beautiful chord? Tolkien was talking about the life, death, resurrection and return of Christ. For Tolkien, Jesus is the *shalom bringer.* Jesus is going to be the "rooftop concert" at the climax of the world's chaos. He's going to make everything sad untrue. And instead of a farewell tour, it'll be Jesus's final arrival.

Shalom on earth. Forever.

It's about the restoration of transcendent harmony to the earth.

And that *is* good news.

THE KINGDOM OF SHALOM

Now, I want to be clear about something. It's not as though Isaiah or Luke or Paul (or Tolkien for that matter) is treating Jesus like an employee at a gas station, who's here to take the earth and "fill 'er up" to get the world back to the way it should be. He's not merely doing us a service, because Jesus is the *entire point* of the world we live in. The beating heart at the center of shalom is God Himself. He is the Great Conductor, and He is the *subject* of the symphony.

So on the one hand, we need to avoid the gospel of escape—"Creation doesn't matter. We need to leave the world." That narrative profanes the good creation God made. But on the other hand, we need to avoid the gospel of paganism—"God is our instrument for making the world the way we want it!" Rather, the gospel is about the *remarriage* of God and humanity. God is not behind the scenes but center stage with His bride, through Christ.

I believe if we evangelicals can recapture the gospel of shalom, our hearts can beat like Jesus's. We did it once. We can do it again. The rest of this book is going to show us how Zechariah's vision can lead us out of the evangelical ruts we're stuck in and into something that gives us a twinkle in the eye: hope. That's because when Jesus talks about the "kingdom of God," He's promising an era of shalom. As Luke's gospel continues, Jesus goes out of His way to show us His kingdom isn't just some distant reality we all need to twiddle our thumbs and wait for. And it's certainly not an earthly political kingdom that can be established, right now, by our power. Rather, it's an already-present reality we can *experience, embody,* and *extend* into the world, here and now.

Jesus says you and I can *experience* God's kingdom of shalom:

> Jesus called the children to him and said, "Let the little children come to me, and do not hinder them, for the kingdom of God belongs to such as these. Truly I tell you, anyone who will not receive the kingdom of God like a little child will never enter it." (Luke 18:16–17)

Jesus says you and I can *embody* God's kingdom of shalom:

> Once, on being asked by the Pharisees when the kingdom of God would come, Jesus replied, "The coming of the kingdom of God is not something that can be observed, nor will people say, 'Here it is,' or 'There it is,' because the kingdom of God is in your midst." (17:20–21)

Jesus says we can *extend* God's kingdom of shalom:

> No one lights a lamp and puts it in a place where it will be hidden, or under a bowl. Instead they put it on its stand, so that those who come in may see the light. (11:33)

As we do these things, Jesus says, His kingdom will grow . . . not through a political coup or force. Rather, it will be like an organic, luscious tree or the probiotic yeast in bread:

> Jesus asked, "What is the kingdom of God like? What shall I compare it to? It is like a mustard seed, which a man took

and planted in his garden. It grew and became a tree, and the birds perched in its branches."

Again he asked, "What shall I compare the kingdom of God to? It is like yeast that a woman took and mixed into about sixty pounds of flour until it worked all through the dough." (13:18–21)

Jesus's vision isn't the doom and gloom we evangelicals believe. It's a vision of a kingdom growing slowly and counterintuitively through history. And here are the facts: Jesus's kingdom has seen more incredible, worldwide growth in the past century than in any century in history. The world we live in today—a world with hospitals, education systems, and a commitment to end slavery—is a world inconceivable to the Greco-Roman Empire of Jesus's day. It all stems from Jesus's wisdom, beauty, and justice filling the world, just like He promised. Those little birds Jesus referred to in the parable above? That's a Jewish picture for the nations—us—flocking into the kingdom of God as it flourishes.

This is so key. Jesus does not picture the kingdom of God shrinking and shrinking until we meet some apocalyptic doomsday and then are evacuated from the earth. Jesus pictures the kingdom of God growing and growing—not through power and politics but through the kind of organic growth you see in the yeast of bread or the seed of a tree as we each experience, embody, and extend His kingdom toward others.

So, fellow evangelicals, do we believe Jesus's kingdom is something we can participate in here and now? Do we believe His kingdom is growing—and has been growing for the past two thousand years—like He promised? We did, once. We can do it again, if we recapture Jesus's dreams.

PART 3

JESUS'S DREAMS

10

Love

We love men not because we like them, nor because their ways appeal to us, nor even because they possess some type of divine spark; we love every man because God loves him.

—DR. MARTIN LUTHER KING, "Strength to Love"

When we step into the pages of the Scriptures, we're all immigrants.

—REBECCA MCLAUGHLIN, *The Secular Creed*

I remember the first time I saw an evangelical express the radical nature of Jesus's hospitality. I was new to a ministry organization called Reformed University Fellowship (RUF). We were at a hotel in Denver, Colorado, the same week a large realty firm was there. That meant lots of highly inebriated, stressed-out business people were letting loose and having a *very* good time. I wasn't judging these people or anything, but I did feel annoyed at them. And also I was definitely judging them. I did everything I could to avoid them all weekend, especially on the elevators. That's because, as a pastor, I carry around this lingering guilt for not sharing the gospel during people's most awkward moments: sitting on an airplane, waiting alone at a hospital, standing on an elevator, whatever. I was trying to do everything I could to avoid that feeling. But late one night, I was taking the elevator with my friend Cool Chris. Cool Chris is a tall, handsome guy who became a Christian in college. He is also just very cool. That's not a good word for a writer to use, but it's true. Everyone who meets him wants to get on his good side, and I was no exception.

As we stood on the elevator together, an older realtor stumbled in with us. His cheeks were cherry red, and his collar was ruffled. He was loud. He smelled like money.

"What's RUF?" he said, reading our name tags. This was doubly annoying to me, because he pronounced it like the sound a dog makes, not like the acronym, which is a self-inflicted wound on our part I know, but *still.*

"We're a ministry," I mumbled. I was trying to politely dismiss him, but Cool Chris was looking directly into the eyes of the drunk realtor.

"We work with college students," Cool Chris clarified. "All of us here are on different campuses around the country, and we're pastors. We try to introduce them to Jesus by getting lunch or coffee with them or by teaching or leading Bible studies." The drunk realtor laughed.

"Well," he said, "I bet you guys aren't drinking, then!"

I tried to make a dumb joke about how we weren't Baptists. Cool Chris asked him how his weekend was going. He asked about the man's business. The man rambled. Cool Chris nodded patiently and kept looking him in the eyes.

The elevator dinged.

"I'mma needa talk to a pastor after this crazy weekend," said the realtor. I gave a courtesy laugh, still trying to shake the guy.

"Any of us would be very happy to talk to you anytime this weekend," Cool Chris said, offering the man a warm smile.

Cool Chris left after the next floor.

I stood alone in the elevator, feeling ashamed.

Why had I been so mean-spirited toward that man? Lying in bed, I had to face the truth about myself: I thought I was better than he was. I wasn't identifying with his humanity or his struggles. My friend Chris did not think he was better than this man. He saw himself in him. It's as though he were saying, "Beneath all that wealth and liquor, I see a man in you, deserving of dignity and respect." He treated him like God's image bearer.

On the elevator, I was being judgmental and tribal. "You're not like us, so I don't like you."

Chris, on the other hand, was offering the hospitality of Jesus.

POP THERAPY VERSUS HOSPITALITY

Growing up, I always thought being loved meant becoming the same as the people around me. To illustrate, imagine a little boy who was always the Frisbee captain at recess and the first pick in team sports. His world was filled with summer camps, posh clothes, and Ivy League–educated aunts and uncles. Imagine a golden child who always won the school lotteries and broke records and whose yearbook picture stood out among his peers for his white teeth and handsome, perfectly quaffed hair. Got the picture? Good. Now imagine the exact opposite of that child, because the opposite of that kid was *me*. I was pudgy and weird and had a bowl cut and wore Looney Tunes clothes everywhere I went. The kid I was describing above was Michael Brown. He was perfect. Whatever kind of human I was, I was the antithesis of Michael.

He and I seemed to exist in different worlds. My family is not an Ivy League family. We were the kind of family who watched Thursday night sitcoms while Michael was doing his honors homework. We were loud, and all my six siblings were hilarious except for one. We held poker tournaments, rode our dirt bikes around other people's property, and bowhunted for our own food in the fall, and the adults drank plenty of cheap beer.

When I go home, those are still the things I love to do. It's in my blood. But I've always thought my family's culture was captured best by our opinions about pizza. Brighton, Michigan, had to have at least thirty pizza places while I was growing up. We tried them all. We *hated* them all. No, we tried them so that we *could* hate them. We made our own pizza—McDonald family pizza. I'm biased, I know, but it really *was* better. It was us against them. The underdog versus the Man. Who was the Man? People like Michael Brown. Left-wing politicians. Big Pizza.

Over the years, I've thought more about the gap between me and Michael Brown. Our families would never be friends. We didn't want to be. They would vote left; we would vote right. He would go to Ivy League schools; I would have fun. We would eat McDonald pizza; he would eat sorry, soggy, pizza his parents paid top dollar for. We might as well have lived on different planets. Why? Because community, in our country, is so often formed around sameness: same class, same schools, same skin color, same religion, same political opinions. "I love you because you're like me" or "I hate you because you're not like me." This is because, for both the Left and the Right, we have a *therapeutic* version of love: Love is about surrounding myself with people who make me feel good.

By critiquing therapeutic love, I don't mean that people shouldn't pursue good, qualified therapists. I think far more of us—especially evangelicals—should do that. I've benefited immensely from good, qualified counselors. By "therapeutic love," I mean what the cultural critic Freddie deBoer—an author who, like me, is in weekly therapy himself—describes as the baseline assumption of the pop-therapeutic world of social media and reputable news sources alike: "The only criteria for deciding whether a behavior is worth doing is the individual's own emotional comfort." Critiquing a popular *New York Times* article that evaluates the merits of forgiveness by assessing whether forgiveness makes people happier, deBoer argues that this way of thinking is going to make us an impossibly selfish society:

> This [article's] implicit value system would justify saying that compassion is good because it reduces blood pressure, that honesty is good because speaking the truth causes a pleasant release of endorphins, that you shouldn't rob and murder someone because doing so might worsen fine lines and wrinkles. It's a stance on morality that has completely excised the interests of others, which is to say, an antimorality, a consumer product marketed in moral terms, a justification for selfishness bought off the rack.[1]

Freddie deBoer is no friend of the Christian worldview or Christian ethics. Yet I think he accurately holds a plumb line to the kind of ethic that evaluates all choices based on our own happiness. In this worldview, he points out, our lives become molded to just the shape we like, and if others can't fit into that shape, well, much the worse for them. This is the wedge that drives the increasing polarization of our country. It's toxicity masking itself as anti-toxicity. Love means becoming the same as me. Fitting my mold. If you can't do that, we can't be friends. And this kind of self-love has no room for sacrificial love. So, yes, I think the Christian worldview has *all the space in the world for good therapy*. The problem is, the pop-therapeutic worldview has *no space for Christianity.* Or, as deBoer argues, ethics in general.

Growing up in a family of addicts of various stripes, I can tell you that this kind of love—the pop-therapeutic love that prizes emotional comfort and validation above all—is what people want *when they hate themselves.* Addicts push away the people who say, "Hey, I think you need help"—the people who truly love them—and they surround themselves with people who affirm all their choices. Addicts can't imagine a kind of love that could name what is broken and *still* love and move toward them. So they run away from people who try to love them and surround themselves with people who make them feel good but ultimately don't give a rip about their self-destructive choices.

I'm as subject to this way of thinking about life as anyone. I live with these assumptions just like you do. I remember seeing this clearly one night while watching a weird film called *Birdman or (The Unexpected Virtue of Ignorance).* It's a movie about a washed-up actor trying to recover his career by writing and performing in a Broadway play adapted from Raymond Carver's short story "What We Talk About When We Talk About Love." In the middle of the film, the has-been actor, Riggan Thomson, has a conversation with his ex-wife and asks, "Why did we break up?" She tells him it's because he threw a kitchen knife at her and then tried to tell her that he loved her. He's not buying it. Finally, she says, "You know, just because I didn't like that ridiculous comedy you did with Goldie Hawn did not mean I did not love you. That's what you always do. You confuse love for admiration."[2]

You confuse love for admiration. When I heard that line, it felt like a punch in the gut. Do I do that? Oh yes. Yes, I do. Every day. Every hour. It could be the billboard for our social media–saturated generation. We confuse love for admiration.

Likes and cheap, meaningless catchphrases become a zombie substitute for the love we're really looking for, deep down: Jesus's love.

Not therapeutic love.

Hospitable love.

JESUS'S PRIESTLY MINISTRY OF LOVE

Jesus's priestly ministry of love is the first thing our friend Zechariah sings about, when he sings about Jesus's dreams:

> You, my child, will be called a prophet of the Most High;
> for you will go on before the Lord to prepare the
> way for him,
> to give his people the knowledge of salvation
> through the forgiveness of their sins,
> because of the tender mercy of our God. (Luke 1:76–78)

The word that's used to describe mercy—*tender*—is *splanchna*.[3] And the original meaning is a bit punchier than our translation. It literally means *guts*. For example, Judas hung himself in a field, and "there he fell headlong, his body burst open and all his *splanchna* spilled out" (Acts 1:18). Pretty gross, huh? I want you to hear the drama of this word, *splanchna*. It is an arresting nausea. A sinking stomach. It's a rare word, meant for expressing the strongest of reactions to someone or something. *Splanchna* was used twice to describe Jesus's compassion for people. Once when He saw people being abused by spiritual leaders—"When he saw the crowds, he had *splanchna* on them, because they were harassed and helpless, like sheep without a shepherd" (Matthew 9:36). And once when Jesus saw people without food—"He had *splanchna* on them and healed their sick" (Matthew 14:14).

But Zechariah says this is how God feels about all of us. He feels not just mercy but *splanchna* mercy for us. Gut-wrenching mercy.

The phrase "tender mercy" tells us two things. The first is that we are incalculably valuable to God. Nobody feels *splanchna* over spilled milk. At some point while writing this book, in a freak accident, I lost about a month's worth of heavy work I'd done. The moment I realized it was gone, I did something I thought people did only in the movies or in the Bible: I ripped my shirt in half. I didn't know such a thing could be done. I don't know why I did it or how. It was a gut-level instinct about something so precious to me, lost. It rose from my innards out into my arms and across my wardrobe— *splanchna.* That's because what I'd been writing was so close to my heart. In a more devastating way, when my brother Joseph drowned, I woke up every morning feeling sick to my stomach, wondering whether it was all a terrible nightmare— *splanchna.* That's because my little brother was incalculably valuable to me.

But that gut-wrenching feeling of "tender mercy" also speaks of a second truth: For Jesus to feel it, something must be radically wrong. When Jesus sees each of us, both things are true. He considers us incalculably valuable. If not, He wouldn't have died for us! But also He sees there is something radically—deadly—wrong in each one of us. If He didn't see that, He wouldn't have died for us. If we're honest with ourselves, we know we need more than just a community of people giving us enabling pats on the back. What we need is to be rescued from the deadly, self-centered story we're all telling ourselves. Even if you don't believe in God, the absurd human intuition to treat the entire world like it's a story about "me" feels—at the very least—like a serious evolutionary malfunction, doesn't it? If you don't believe me, google any beautiful ancient landmark. Last week, I plugged "the Dead Sea" into Google Maps.

Here's what popped up: "The Dead Sea . . . 4.4 stars."

So. You're telling me a bunch of people walked up to an ancient body of water and . . . *generally rated it 4 out of 5 stars?* I started scrolling through the reviews. It was worse. Some people rated it 3 stars or 1 star. Well, *I'm sorry,* people, but that is the actual Dead Sea, you know. Did you expect a different Dead Sea? Have you seen a better one? It made me wonder what the Dead Sea would say if it could rate us.

"Insignificant future piles of sand who think they're the center of the universe. *One star.*"

What a weird, totally senseless way to think about the world. The most important thing about an ancient landmark is our personal experience of it. We get to rate it on our own scale of satisfaction. This is crazy. Seeing ourselves—and our ratings, opinions, and otherwise—as the center of a billions-of-light-years-wide universe is just a little absurd. But that's the way all of us are. That's a silly example, of course. But multiply that out into the entire human experience, and you have the cacophony of noise, chaos, and war Tolkien wrote about, as we discussed in the previous chapter. This chaos is what Scripture calls *death.* The reason we're not living in shalom—the reason we live in a world full of death—is because of this poisonous, self-centered instinct to make the world's orchestra a solo about *us.* And yet, when God looks at us, says Zechariah, He says, "My heart goes out to you."

God knows you're a difficult person.

How does He respond?

In His famous story about the prodigal son, Jesus speaks of a punk kid who wishes his father were dead. He has his father cut a check, wastes the entire fortune on women, booze, and fun, and then comes crawling back to his father.

The father's response?

"His father saw him and was filled with compassion [*splanchna*] for him; he ran to his son, threw his arms around him and kissed him" (Luke 15:20).

Splanchna.

Jesus is asking, "You want to know how God feels about you? He feels like that dad. *Splanchna.*" This kind of love—tender mercy—is the only kind of love that can transform you and me to become people who love beyond our tribes.

This story hit home for me in the strangest way, once again, while I sat watching yet another weird film called *Pig,* starring Nicolas Cage. It's about a famous retired chef living in the woods with his truffle pig. Together, they scout for rare truffles and sell them for just enough to get by. Then, one night, the truffle pig disappears. It's been stolen.

Now, this is a classic setup for a revenge film—think Liam Neeson's *Taken,* Denzel Washington's *Man on Fire,* Mel Gibson's *Braveheart,* Shakespeare's *Hamlet.* At this point in the movie, our blood is rising and we're ready for guns and swords and, I guess, in Hamlet's case, some pouty existential meditations. So Nicolas Cage walks into the city . . . and enters a fight club.

Of course he does.

Cage stands in the middle of the arena, unmoving. A small man, grinning, rises to fight. After a bit of dancing, the small man lands a blow to Cage's jaw. Cage doesn't respond. The man lands another.

And another.

And another.

Cage, now beaten and breathless, continues to look the small man in the eye. The man laughs with glee as Cage falls to the ground, and he strikes Cage's face again and again. It's a sickening scene. But as we see Cage being beaten, we also see the reaction of the crowd. By the end of the fight, the onlookers don't seem entertained. Instead, they appear horror-stricken and have tears in their eyes—the greatest chef their city has ever known has just been beaten to a bloody pulp before them. At the end of the fight, one of the onlookers hands Cage a paper, telling him exactly who to ask to find his truffle pig.

Cage continues to wander the city, placing himself in vulnerable positions. He plays drums with a little boy. He enters the pretentious restaurant of one of his former line cooks, shares a glass of wine with him, and reminds the line cook of his young dream: not to please critics but to open a pub. The man breaks down in tears and tells Cage exactly where to go to find his pig. The entire last third of the film shows us Nicolas Cage preparing an elaborate, heartfelt meal, every single ingredient filled with inspired meaning—for the man he thinks is ultimately responsible for stealing his truffle pig. As the meal is being prepared, we see the hardened villain's crusty exterior begin to crack and then fold. I won't spoil the ending.[4]

What's going on in this strange film? It's a movie about the transformative power of *hospitable love.* Cage doesn't pat his enemies on the back and affirm all their choices. He doesn't throw his hands up and walk away. Rather, he looks them each in the eye and says, "Let me remind you of what is beautiful in life. Let me show you the meaning of love. Let me serve you a meal." This film is a parable of Jesus's love for you, reader. Jesus's priestly ministry is simply this: He came to your place. He walked around in your shoes. He took on your self-centered mess on the cross. He looks you straight in the eye and sets a table for you: His body and blood. He loves who you are now—not a worthless worm, not a flawless saint, but a dangerously flawed yet incalculably valuable creation of His. He made you what you are. He wants you to let His hospitable love transform you into the person you were meant to be. This is why those of us who've experienced Jesus's hospitable love don't say, "I'm good, and you're bad."

We say, "I'm loved, and you are too."

This is Jesus's first and highest dream for you: That you might experience His love.

That you might embody that love in a community.

That you might extend that love to others.

EXPERIENCING JESUS'S LOVE: THE PRACTICE OF COMMUNION

When I think of *experiencing* Jesus's love, I think of my friend Joseph.

When I first met him, Joseph scared me because he is very muscular and intelligent and serious-looking. Sometimes I'll say something I think sounds intelligent, and Joseph will say, "Why do you say that?" with a sharp look that makes me think about excusing myself to the bathroom at the bagel shop we meet at and then crawling into the ventilator and escaping like they do in the movies. But actually, Joseph is an incredibly kind, generous person who loves people with *splanchna* love. That's because, after college, he found himself deconstructing his evangelical experience growing up. Through the 2016 election, Black Lives Matter, and other cultural events, his friends—who had served alongside him in a thriving ministry space—began to question their convictions. When the evangelical spaces around him started echoing things he'd experienced as a minority in his Christian high school, Joseph started to wonder whether he was in the right space. I asked him to share a bit about his own journey, and here's what he told me.

"All childhoods contain good and bad. Mine, in and around a Southern Baptist megachurch, had more than its fair share of good, but the difficulties made a stronger impression on my view of Christianity. Casual racism and moral hypocrisy made me view God as possessing dubious levels of trustworthiness and goodness. Lack of intellectual and theological depth left me with questions, doubts, and a simplistic view of salvation as an algebraic atonement equation of sin + grace = eternal life, which was described as an undying existence in the clouds with golden harps."

Joseph grew up around a theology of escape. It was a theology that told him his body and his culture didn't matter to Jesus. Because of that, Jesus's love was a pure abstraction. Joseph continued, "I graduated college wrestling with philosophical doubts and dysfunctional emotions stemming from my clouded view of God. I coped with bouts of depression and anxiety by chasing knowledge, a prime candidate for deconstructing my faith. I was convinced that if I built the correct mental framework for philosophy and theology, then I would be able to move through life in security, safety, and confidence."

Around that time, nearly all Joseph's friends deconstructed their faith and left the church. He found himself drowning in all the information surrounding him in books, podcasts, and angry rants from friends. But Joseph also did something his deconstructing friends didn't do. He started worshipping on Sundays at Redeemer, the church I help pastor. He shared,

Redeemer was different from anything I'd experienced. Every week, we got on our knees and confessed our sin. I recognized myself in those prayers. Then you guys pronounced Jesus's forgiveness over me every week. And every single week, I took communion. I'd never done that before. Every week a pastor or elder would administer communion to me, look me in the eyes, and tell me that Jesus loved me. This all did something for my heart that I didn't even know I needed. Most weeks I arrived at church wrestling with bitterness, disappointment, shame, sin, and discontent; I cannot remember a single week where I left without a happy heart.

While my intellectual questions were important (and there are answers) and my emotional battles real, my primary need was the gospel—not as a detached abstract theory or an algebra equation but as something communal, embodied, beautiful, received. The question behind my questions was "Can I trust God?" And experiencing Jesus through confession and assurance, and taking communion every week, answered that question for me. Eventually, my questions became . . . quieter. I found answers, and good answers. But as it turns out, my biggest question was "Am I loved by Jesus?" Experiencing His mercy in an embodied way every week answered that question for me. That's made all the difference.

According to Luke, in the earliest days of the church, communion was seen as the climax of the weekly gathering: "On the first day of the week we came together *to break bread*" (Acts 20:7). It's striking that Luke can describe the very purpose of an early-church worship service in these terms: We came together in order to enjoy communion together. In fact, surprising as it seems, the weekly "love feasts" of Christians— where the church gathered to celebrate the priestly love of Jesus through a meal—was one of Roman society's main objections to the new faith. No one could understand how such deep, abiding, and intimate love could be anything other than erotic.[5] They simply had no category for Jesus's hospitable love.

Why did we get away from this weekly (and possibly daily)[6] practice of communion? There are all sorts of historical twists and turns to the story. But at the very least, one reason we no longer see the Lord's table as vital to our spiritual health is our theology of escape. If our spirits matter but our bodies don't, then all we really need from Sunday mornings is some great intellectual content from a sermon, right? But as Joseph said above, the intellectual answers weren't enough. The created *imago Dei* part of Joseph was craving something more. Taking communion every week healed his heart, even as he tried to figure out the intellectual answers to his questions. This isn't to diminish at all the vital role of hearing God's Word week in and week out (which we'll talk about in the next chapter). But Joseph needed both. That's because the ancient practice of participating in the Lord's table is how we're meant to experience the physical, touchable proof that Jesus, our Priest, is *with* us. Sometimes I meet younger people wrestling with whether they really belong to Jesus or not. "Am I really a Christian? Am I saved?" they ask. Often these young people are told, "Once you're saved, you're always saved," or they're given some other kind of theological answer to their questions. It never seems to help. But historic Christians would have responded much differently to these doubts. They would have said, "If you want to be assured of your faith . . . *lean into the Lord's table.*" Consider the beautiful Heidelberg Catechism's pastoral answer to those who doubt Jesus's promises and love for them:

> First, as surely as I see with my eyes the bread of the Lord broken for me and the cup shared with me, so surely his body was offered and broken for me and his blood poured out for me on the cross. Second, as surely as I receive from the hand of the one who serves, and taste with my mouth the bread and cup of the Lord, given me as sure signs of

Christ's body and blood, so surely he nourishes and refreshes my soul for eternal life with his crucified body and poured-out blood.[7]

Would you like to be assured of Jesus's love for you? Touch it. Taste it. Drink it. Experience it. Each week when the leaders Jesus entrusted with our care hand us bread and wine, they're saying, "Whether you feel it or not, Jesus's promise of faithfulness to you is as real as the bread and wine. You can taste it. You can touch it. He loves your body and your soul. Here's proof." This is, as my pastor friend Sam likes to say, the hug of Jesus. The Lord's table is the place where we learn to live each day into being *beloved* by Christ. This habit begins in worship together, but it spreads outward. The ancient word for communion, *eucharist,* literally means "thanksgiving." So the invitation to communion is the invitation to see life and creation, each day, as a gift given to you by a Jesus whose heart bleeds for you.

EMBODYING JESUS'S LOVE: THE PRACTICE OF CONFESSION

When I think of *embodying* Jesus's love, I think of the RUF pastors I was privileged to work with for several years.

During my time at RUF, I noticed that the pastors never said things like "We're all sinners." It's not that they didn't believe that. But for them, that was too abstract. Too hypothetical. Instead, they'd say things like this:

"I just had an argument with my wife and I'm in a pissy mood."

"I drank too much last night."

"I don't feel like I believe in Jesus this month."

Wow, I thought at first. *These guys are pretty bad Christians.* But these pretty bad Christians were also the Christians who put me to shame for the way they loved drunk businessmen, hungover students who needed hospital rides at 1:00 A.M., and freshmen who used them as emotional punching bags for their daddy issues. These men and women were so patient and kind. They could look these "others" in the eye with love. And I couldn't. I was judgmental. Angry. Self-righteous. After some time, I came to see the connection: I thought of myself only as a *hypothetical* sinner, not as an *actual* sinner. If you asked me, "Are you a sinner?" I could say, "Of course." But if you asked "How?" that would have offended me. That's because *sinner* had come to be an abstraction to me, a hypothetical. Now that I was saved—and a pastor, no less!—it was rude of anyone to think I was an *actual* sinner.

But I realized there was a golden thread between the raw, vulnerable confessions of my RUF pastor friends and their deep, warm hospitality to others. There was a crusty barrier between the kind of love I had for the drunk businessman and the kind of love they had. Because my sin was only "hypothetical," Jesus's love for me was *also* hypothetical. By denying my daily, actual sin, I was simultaneously denying my daily, actual need for Jesus's radical mercy for me. Jesus's love for me, then, was a purely abstract idea. I didn't understand it deep in my bones like my friend Cool Chris. And that's why I couldn't extend it to the drunk realtor. We evangelicals talk gobs about sin and how we're all sinners and how we all need Jesus. But I had never seen any evangelical leaders I knew freely talk about themselves like they were *actual* sinners. And that sent a clear message: We don't believe we're actually sinners. We believe we *used to be* sinners, which means Jesus *used to have* radical love for us. And if that hasn't cleaned us up by now, He's pretty much done with us. This kind of love won't transform any of us into the kinds of people Jesus dreams for us to be.

What the men and women in RUF showed me was that Jesus's love was not a onetime event. Confession isn't just a moment in time where we change from sinners to Christians. Embodying Jesus's hospitable love requires daily and weekly *confession* of our sin in a safe, gospel-transformed community. This is why I've delighted in the every-Sunday practice of confessing sin together at Redeemer. Just to give you a taste of this experience, here is a recent confession we did as a congregation:

All: We trust in our family,
   our upbringing,
   our education,
   our gifts and abilities,
   our privilege,
   our jobs and net worth,
to keep us safe, to deliver us, to make us acceptable.

Leader: At times we feel covered in shame, like we're worthless,
   which gives a seedbed for sin.

All: In shame we isolate and disconnect from people;
   we hide in darkness and secrets.
We buy the lie that we deserve to be alone,
   that God doesn't want us.
Then, like our first parents, we cover our shame with fig leaves,
   rather than turn to our maker and redeemer.

Leader: Father, Son, and Spirit, we call out to you!

All: Hear our cry for mercy![8]

Ouch. But here's the beautiful thing. After this confession, I (or another pastor at Redeemer) get to stand up and joyfully declare that Jesus loves every single person in that room and is running toward them with open arms.

Years ago, before I became a pastor at Redeemer, I had a friend who stopped going to church for some time. When he ended up back in a church—a church that in my shallow opinion didn't have enough slickness to its presentation—I asked him why he felt so compelled by his little church. Without skipping a beat, he said, "The confession and assurance. I know I'll hear I'm forgiven every week. I need that." What a beautiful picture of being Jesus's disciple.

But the practice of confession isn't meant to stop here. As Jesus's brother James wrote, "Confess your sins to each other and pray for each other so that you may be healed" (5:16). Confession may begin in worship together. But to confess is to bring out what is truly inside us in our relationships with others. That can mean confessing our wrongdoings to one another. It can also mean confessing our needs and desires to one another, something I find far harder to do than simply saying, "I was wrong." So while we may begin by confessing together on a Sunday, this confession is meant to invite us into a deeper web of relationships where we regularly reveal what is inside us and receive the healing James spoke of.

My biker friend Bill, who converted to Roman Catholicism several years ago, likes to tease me about this point. He says Protestants can't follow the command to confess because they don't have a priest to confess their sins to. I remind him that confession would be a lot easier for me if the guy I was confessing to was locked in a booth. I've got to live with these people I confess to, day in and day out! But Bill the Biker's point is largely true. Most evangelicals don't confess their sin to one another . . . at all. We're happy to have high-minded

Bible studies and listen to all the high-minded sermons, but we hardly ever make space to confess our personal, individual sins to one another. The transforming power of Jesus's mercy becomes stunted in our daily lives because we've never truly embodied it in community.

My recovering-alcoholic friend Tim likes to say, "Everyone wants a private healing. We all want recovery from our bad habits privately. But when I read the Gospels, I don't see a single private healing." The key to healing, says Tim, is confession. Weekly. In groups. With one another. Our sins. Our hopes. Our needs and desires. Our faith. It's only then that we can be a community that embodies Jesus's merciful hospitality. Of all the practices in this book, this is where I need to grow the most. But since my encounter with RUF, I find myself doing "micro-confessions" all over the place—to strangers, non-Christians, anyone who cares to listen. I always thought it was a bad idea to tell non-Christians about my sins, because they'd have no reason to become Christians after that. But the weird thing is, the non-Christians I know are actually incredibly intrigued and compelled by this kind of confession. They see I have a security that they can't find anywhere else: the transforming safety of Jesus's mercy to me.

EXTENDING JESUS'S LOVE: THE PRACTICE OF HOSPITALITY

When I think of *extending* Jesus's love, I think of my friend Luke the Dirt Scientist.

Luke the Dirt Scientist and I met one day at the student center at the University of Missouri. It was my first year on campus as an RUF pastor, and I had set up a table full of candy out in the lobby and told myself no matter how awkward it felt, I'd smile at every single student that passed. After three hours, the best I'd done was get into a debate with a

Jewish student about the Old Testament sacrificial system, and for some reason this did not make him want to be part of my ministry.

Then, for whatever reason, I locked eyes with a student across the room. He headed my way—to this day he couldn't tell you why—and we hit it off. He talked about growing up in a progressive church in Kansas City, but since they didn't take the Bible seriously, it felt to him more like a social and political club. Here's Luke in his own words:

> I grew up the grandson of a Southern Baptist preacher, but throughout my formative years we attended a very progressive Methodist church. My youth group was interested in social justice—we did a sermon series on becoming "social justice warriors" before the phrase got baggage. We were pretty light on doctrinal teaching. When I and other students would ask my youth pastor deep questions ("Is Christianity the only right religion?" etc.) later in high school, he had a half-assed answer to all of it that framed Christianity as the most true of many religions that related to God in different ways.

By the time I met Luke, he'd checked out of church.

Our first conversation went so well. I said, "Hey, we have a freshman Bible study next Monday. Want to join?"

"I'll be there," said Luke. These are not words you typically hear from college students.

Did we have a freshman Bible study the next Monday, you ask? That didn't matter. The point is, we had one now. I frantically texted all the freshmen I knew and told them so. And that study continued throughout the semester, with Luke showing up regularly. Now, I loved my freshman students very much, but they weren't exactly the most social bunch of people I'd ever met. So at the end of the semester, I told them that it was really cool how they liked to meet together to study the Bible—like, *really* cool—but that it would also be really cool if they, you know . . . just hung out with one another. Without studying the Bible. They wanted to know why.

"Because that's normal," I said. "Look, I'll even organize it for you. Let's plan a night where we hang out."

Someone suggested making pizzas at my house, which I thought was a great idea. So we bought some things to make pizzas and invited our freshmen over for a party at our house. Out of a deep and abiding sense of piety and moral duty, they attended. The night, I felt, was a bit strange. Some students talked about their homework. One student in the corner would talk only to my dog. Our house was very . . . quiet. I thought maybe Luke the Dirt Scientist, who joined us, would decide right then and there that he wasn't so interested in Christianity after all. But Luke seemed fine, and . . . he kept coming. After several months—through this Bible study, on-campus sermons, and our church at the time (Christ Our King)—Luke the Dirt Scientist became a Christian. He's several years out from college now, but reflecting on that time, he shared,

> Growing up, I'm not sure I ever learned the gospel, the good news that Christ has risen from the dead and sits at the right hand of the Father where He reigns with the Spirit over the heavens and the earth. The emphasis the faith of my youth put on performance is something I'm working through in my spiritual, relational, and professional life. The grace of God saving me through no power of myself has been unravelling this within me—the greatest things I've received in life I did not and could never earn. Eternal life, the friendship of Christ, the love of my bride, the warm embrace of the church. All grace.

How did Luke receive this profound understanding of Jesus's love toward him? That's what I asked him one day during his senior year in the cafeteria over stir-fry. I wanted to know what exactly had recaptured his interest in Christianity and compelled him to seek out Jesus for answers. I was thinking of a couple of really great sermons I'd done and about how I'd led some very excellent Bible studies with him and about some profound apologetics points I had explained when we were arguing about Christianity. And do you know what he said?

"It was probably the night we made pizzas at your house. It was just a few of us, and it was super awkward, but I loved it."

Luke must have misheard my question.

"Um, no," I said. "I asked you what really helped you become a *Christian.* You know like a sermon I preached or something. Or something I said. Or something profound I wrote to you."

"No, that was it. The pizzas. Obviously hearing about Jesus was key. But when we made pizzas at your house, I thought, *I'm in. This is what I'm looking for.*"

For Luke, the merciful love of Jesus *extended* through a simple feast—a few of us making pizzas at our house one night—demonstrated the power of the gospel to him. We were an oddball bunch, to be sure. But Luke saw that only the transformative, hospitable, merciful love of Jesus could make our little ragtag community possible. He wasn't going to find that anywhere else, and it compelled him into our church's doors months later, where he was introduced to the source of that love: Jesus's mercy. It's lovely to see the way this kind of hospitality works out in Luke's own life today.

"The gospel," Luke said, "has transformed how I interact with others and myself. It has brought my mind more peace— God has revealed things in my heart and embraces me every morning so I can embrace others." He shared about his work as an environmental scientist and how, through the church, he's rubbed shoulders with people his industry considers "the bad guys":

> In college, I did a summer internship at a church in Texas where I lived with an oil executive. Guys like him are "the evil overlords" in the climate story. But this guy's family was so kind to me, I can't believe that story. It humanized someone I'm supposed to think is morally backward. This helps me do good work, because you can't help people who you despise. So, at my job I am able to see where folks are coming from—serious, competent people who are sometimes scared about what change might do to the organizations they have built their careers and lives upon—and help them.

If you want to be part of extending Jesus's love to others, start with a meal. Food is the universal language of intimacy. This is why the religious leaders were so offended at Jesus's sharing meals with others (Luke 15:2). It's why the first interaction Jesus had with Peter after his betrayal began with Jesus inviting him to breakfast on the beach (John 21). It's why Jesus promises to hold a banquet for us in the new heavens and earth (Luke 14:15–24). Eating a meal with someone who isn't like us is the clearest way we can imitate Jesus's own life and ministry, which is why showing hospitality—or "stranger love" (the Greek word for "hospitality," *philoxenia*, literally means "love of strangers"[9])—was a requirement for being an early church leader (Titus 1:8). So feasting was meant to point to the rebellious, joyful hope of the Christian faith: We feast now because we will feast in the new heavens and earth, where King Jesus sets the table. But the early church requirement of hospitality for leaders tells us these feasts were also meant to be a place of radical inclusion, where strangers literally tasted the Christian hope for themselves, for the first time. If people are going to take Jesus seriously in our secularizing age, they're going to need Jesus to come to them—the same Jesus who ate so many meals with weirdos and sinners in the Gospels that, as nerdy Lukan scholars like to say, he ate his way right through the book of Luke. That's because eating meals with the different— politically, religiously, sexually—is core to Jesus's ministry. That means it's core to your life and mine. Of course, there may be several other things you need to do before you're ready for a meal with someone different. For example, you may need to become a regular at a coffee shop, take initiative to get to know other parents at your child's school, or join an interest or service group in your community. Hospitality often begins by being faithfully present in public spaces, intentional about your time there, interruptible in your schedule, and caring in your follow-up (do you remember people's names and stories?). Little things, perhaps, to begin.

But this is Jesus's dream of love, coming true.

11

Freedom

The truth will set you free. But not until it is finished with you.

—DAVID FOSTER WALLACE, *Infinite Jest*

Robert Angier: Hasn't good come of your obsessions?
Nikola Tesla: Well, at first. But I followed them too long.
I'm their slave . . . and one day they'll choose to destroy me.

—*THE PRESTIGE (movie)*

I remember the first time I saw an evangelical express the radical nature of Jesus's freedom. It was my job interview with Musical Steve. Musical Steve was a pastor when I met him, but before that he'd been a musician. When Steve and I met, I put on my pastor character, which meant I pretended I wasn't interested in music or movies or anything other than spiritual things. But Steve asked what I studied in college, so I told him.

"I studied . . . film."

I could hear Steve's voice light up over the phone.

"Ooooh, really?" he said. "What kind of film? Who are your favorite directors?" I decided to go with my weirdest choice, which is a creepy, funny director who makes Halloween-themed Claymation Christmas films, as well as films about people with scissors for hands. "Well . . . I really like Tim Burton."

"Aha!" he said. "*Edward Scissorhands* is a favorite of mine. It's all about being an *artist*."

I knew at that moment that Steve was a different kind of pastor. Over the next few years, Steve and I would meet weekly to talk for hours about film, art, literature, the Bible, church history, and what it's like to be a pastor. As quickly as Steve could rejoice with me in the beauty of a John Green novel, he could ferociously defend the beauty and coherence of the Scriptures. Whenever I said something he didn't agree with, I could tell. It wasn't because he barked at me. It's because he smiled at me with a little twinkle in his eye. Most of the time he scribbled everything I said down on a little notepad. He did that for everyone. It's a pretty nerdy way to show someone you care about what they say, but it meant a lot to me. I felt relaxed telling Musical Steve about my passions, artistic thoughts, theological questions, and doubts. Our conversations ran the gamut. One minute we'd be talking about the beauties and flaws of Stephen Sondheim's musicals, and the next we'd be in some obscure historical church argument.

Musical Steve didn't care at all about the culture wars or how I voted or which "side" of the issues I was on. He wasn't with one crowd or the other, but he was happily dogmatic about what the global, historic church believed. He even growled a little bit if he thought I was going astray, and in response I'd call him a fundamentalist, and in response he would smile with a twinkle in his eyes and say, "Of course I'm a fundamentalist. We all have things we consider fundamental to Christian faith. The question is, What are the fundamentals?" Steve was annoying like that. He didn't let me put people in a box. Especially him. But that's because Steve's version of freedom was simple. Everyone is allowed to be themselves. Everyone. But also everyone has to be faithful to the truth. Everyone. That's why, dogmatic and fundamentalist as he was (or so I thought at the time), Musical Steve's small New England congregation was filled with all sorts. He spent time with everybody. Steve loved the Scriptures, but he didn't use them as a weapon. He used them as a flashlight to unearth the beauty around him. Rather than parsing the world into good guys and bad guys, good cultures and bad cultures, Steve just saw the world for what it was: beautiful and flawed. I learned from Musical Steve that light doesn't choose cultural tribes; it illuminates every culture. At Steve's small church, I knew faithful Democrats and Republicans. I knew homeschool families and public-school families. Some of my high school students ended up at Penn State, Harvard, and Yale, while others joined their dad's lumberyard or became social justice warriors in South America or mixed martial artists or parttime musicians. Everyone had their own flavor, their own color.

That's because it was a place made colorful by the light of Jesus.

INCOMPETENCE VERSUS MASTERY

One thing to know about me is that I'm the most stubborn person you've ever met, and you can't convince me otherwise. For instance, once in college, we were debating about where to eat. My friends decided to save money by using up the rest of their meal plans at the cafeteria. I decided to go to Taco John's. My friend Rebekah went ballistic on me.

"That's the thing with you, Nick," she said. "If we're all going to the cafeteria and you want to go to Taco John's, you'll just go to Taco John's by yourself. You'll always do whatever you want to do, no matter what we choose. It's hard to be friends with someone like that."

What she didn't mention is that Taco John's put nice little crispy hash browns in their tacos, giving them an extra crispy crunch, but when I brought this point up to her, it didn't seem to help. I was mad at her at first, but years later I realized she was right. By putting myself—and my own preferences—above everybody else, I was on a dark path toward loneliness and depression. I wasn't free. I was trapped inside myself. I was insisting the world become my silhouette. Why? I thought being my true self meant expressing what was inside me and doing what I pleased without regard for anyone or anything around me. But in my obsession over expressing myself, I was losing touch with who I was meant to be and who my friends—and eventually my family—needed me to be.

The American idea of freedom as self-expressive individualism was parodied in a fantastic *Saturday Night Live* skit about President George Washington rallying his troops to fight the British. They're discouraged, so Washington tries to rouse them by reminding them what they're fighting for: Liberty. Freedom.

WASHINGTON: We fight for a country of our own. A new
   nation where we choose our own laws.
SOLDIERS: Hear! Hear!
WASHINGTON: Choose our own leaders.
SOLDIERS: Yes, sir!
WASHINGTON: And choose our own systems of weights
   and measures.

This statement is met with confusion. For the rest of the skit, Washington goes on to describe the bizarre new systems of weights and measurements we're going to use to replace the historic, global metric system understood by communities around the world.

WASHINGTON: We are free men! And we will be free to
measure liquids in liters and milliliters, but not all liq-
uids, only soda, wine, and alcohol.
SOLDIER: Only those, sir?
WASHINGTON: Yes, because for milk and paint, we will
use gallons, pints, and quarts, God willing. . . .
SOLDIER: Why?
WASHINGTON: *Liberty,* son. *Liberty.*

Then one Black soldier asks him what will become of the
men of color in our liberated country.

WASHINGTON: You asked about the temperature.
BLACK SOLDIER: I did not.[1]

It's a side-splitting skit, so much so that it was called by
some the greatest *SNL* skit of all time. It's poking fun at the
individualistic idea White Americans tend to have about freedom: Freedom is all about me. It's about expressing myself,
doing things my way. I can ignore the needs of the community around me and everything that came before, so long as I
express what's inside me. As historian Jemar Tisby noted, it's
this White, individualistic idea that was a core belief behind
the January 6 insurrection.[2] And the idea of freedom as purely
about self-expression is very different from the Black evangelical conception of freedom, as well as the global, historic
church's idea of freedom. I'd add that it's unaligned with
pretty much any civilization in history, including the Greco-
Roman culture, whose earliest philosophers saw the idea of
"following our hearts" as the antithesis of freedom, since it
meant being ruled by passion.[3] Freedom begins, these philosophers argued, by living with the grain of the universe, not
fighting against it. We experience true freedom, they argued,
when we live from a place of *wisdom.*

I find that the people who understand the connection between wisdom and self-expression are—maybe counterintuitively—my creative friends. My friend Kyle the artist, who you'll meet in the next chapter, is a renowned painter. Whenever I see his work, I know exactly who it belongs to, because it has a certain fantastical whimsy and heartfelt spirituality to it. It reflects the inner world of my friend Kyle so naturally that it would seem to an amateur eye like mine that he can pluck these paintings straight from his soul without effort. Yet Kyle will tell you that the freedom he has to express himself through art comes from decades of studying masters, attending workshops, and practicing techniques. Of course, when I paint, I, too, have a certain kind of freedom—but it's *the freedom of incompetence.* I feel the freedom to paint however I like, simply because I have no idea what I'm doing. The result is chaos. It doesn't express my true self at all. That would require the kind of freedom Kyle has: *the freedom of mastery.*

The same is true of comedians. The very best comedians sound incredibly natural, like they're sitting on your couch with a beer, shooting the breeze. Yet in comedian Steve Martin's autobiography, *Born Standing Up,* he shares how his very "natural" style of comedy was, in fact, the result of thousands of hours analyzing why jokes do and don't work—every bit of syntax, body movement, and voice inflection had been carefully considered.[4] Martin expresses himself naturally *because of* his dedication to the wisdom of his craft, not *in spite of* it. True artists understand that, without wise constraints, art doesn't express anything. It's simply chaos. If an artist wants to express what's deep inside them, they'll need to labor hard to acquire generations of artistic wisdom. The same is true in storytelling or music. One of the most experimental films of the last few decades, *Memento*—which upends us by playing with time from beginning to end—is, according to Christopher Nolan himself, a film that works within the deep constraints of narrative mechanics, based on centuries-old philosophical wisdom.[5] My infant banging on the keys of a piano has *the freedom of incompetence.* He has freedom, but only to create chaos. Gary Hoey, from chapter 9, has spent thousands of hours mastering scales, arpeggios, and technique. He has *the freedom of mastery.* He can express himself fully because he has invested himself in the musical wisdom of the ages. We could go on.

The point is, we can choose to live with the freedom of incompetence: the freedom that doesn't heed the wisdom of the Scriptures, the past, or the people around us. But our lives will simply be an expression of chaos. If we want to express ourselves beautifully, we can't do it by ourselves. True freedom—the kind that allows us to be our truest, most electric selves—comes by experiencing, embodying, and extending the wisdom of Jesus. This is the kind of freedom Jesus described: "If you abide in my word . . . you will know the truth, and the truth will set you free" (John 8:31–32, ESV).

JESUS'S PROPHETIC MINISTRY OF FREEDOM

As Zechariah continued his song, notice what followed just after he sang about God's tender mercy:

You, my child, will be called a prophet of the Most High;
    for you will go on before the Lord to prepare the
        way for him,
to give his people the knowledge of salvation
    through the forgiveness of their sins,
because of the tender mercy of our God,
    by which the rising sun will come to us from heaven
to shine on those living in darkness
    and in the shadow of death. (Luke 1:76–79)

Notice the phrase "by which." God's *splanchna* love is an instrument to deliver something else into our lives. So what is Jesus's mercy delivering to us? *The rising sun.*

Bit of an odd gift, yes?

So let's back up and think about Zechariah's picture of the morning sun. In the Hebrew Scriptures, light is a central image—maybe even *the* central image—for God's relationship to the world. It's the oldest metaphor in the Bible. The Hebrew scriptures open with an image of darkness and light. Light is featured in the first verses of the entire Bible as the first thing God creates (Genesis 1:1–3). Why? Because light is the great life giver. Light warms us and illuminates our world with color. It's the life force that brings forth jungles, rivers, fish, mammals, and flesh and bone. So light, in Genesis 1, means *life* and *flourishing.* The Genesis imagery in Zechariah's song isn't an accident. Zechariah is purposefully using creation language to tell us that Jesus Himself is our sunrise. He will bring new-creation energy into a world filled with darkness. In the same way God spoke creation into existence, so Jesus will—through His words—speak new creation into each of our lives. That new-creation energy, described as the arrival of a sunrise, is what the Scriptures call "freedom." This is why Jesus said, "I am the light of the world. Whoever follows me will not walk in darkness, but will have the light of life. . . . If you abide in *my word,* you are truly my disciples, and you will know the truth, and the truth will set you free" (John 8:12, 31–32, ESV).

The last few weeks, my son Caleb and I have been going to an early-morning meeting with some friends. As we travel through downtown Indianapolis, we see the sunrise together, or more accurately, the sunrise shows us everything around us. These are sweet and quiet moments when we both look around our city and see it in a way we haven't before. As we're driving around, looking at buildings and artwork and gas stations and people, it's like watching everything wake up. It's like watching everything *become itself.* That's the meaning of Zechariah's light imagery. Jesus has come to return the world *back to itself.* To wake it up. He wants His people to be filled with that new-creation energy. Jesus uses two crucial metaphors to make this point: *salt* and *light* (Matthew 5:13–16). It may sound odd to us, but in the Jewish understanding, both of these were seen as life-giving substances. Salt preserves what's good in food it touches, and it strains out what could infect it. Light reveals what's beautiful around us, and it exposes what's dark. This is Jesus's vision of the way we Christians are to wisely engage with the culture around us—not to separate from it, but to preserve its goodness while exposing the darkness. But this kind of wisdom, and freedom, can be found only when Jesus's words are our light.

Jesus tells a short story to make this point. Imagine two men on HGTV, trying to build their dream homes. We'll call them Bob and Jim. Both of them have beautiful designs. Both blueprints perfectly express their aesthetic tastes, their lifestyles, and their care for their families. But as we watch the show continue, we see that Bob is willing to take the TV host's advice. He adjusts his preferences and vision based on her many years of experience and wisdom. The other guy, Jim, not so much. For example, Jim says he wants to build his house in an area of Florida where hurricanes are known to blow through. He loves the ocean view he has in this area. The TV host says, "That's a bad idea. We want you to have an ocean view, but this area is dangerous. It's swampy, for one. And it's prone to hurricane damage." Jim tells her this is his dream. He tells her she needs to let him be himself. "Let me do *me*, okay, lady?" Finally, with a very brief "help me" glance at the camera, the TV host lets Jim have his wish.

Bob takes the advice, and we see him, years later, living a

happy, secure life. But as we fast-forward in Jim's life, we see things have not gone so well. As predicted, building on a swamp created incredible strain on the house Jim was trying to make. Millions of repair dollars later, Jim goes bankrupt. When a particularly bad hurricane blows through, Jim's house is destroyed. Jesus concludes,

> As for everyone who comes to me and hears my words and puts them into practice, I will show you what they are like. They are like a man building a house, who dug down deep and laid the foundation on rock. When a flood came, the torrent struck that house but could not shake it, because it was well built. But the one who hears my words and does not put them into practice is like a man who built a house on the ground without a foundation. The moment the torrent struck that house, it collapsed and its destruction was complete. (Luke 6:47–49)

What's Jesus saying? He's saying that if we want freedom—if we want to be our truest selves, to "build our houses"—then we desperately need His wisdom. Jim's radicalized vision of freedom—total autonomy—ironically leads to captivity and self-destruction. Self-expression isn't the problem. Trying to express ourselves *by ourselves*—without Jesus's creative wisdom—is the problem. Bob isn't suppressing his true self by listening to wisdom; he's able to express himself in a meaningful way *because* his house has a solid foundation of truth. Jim, ironically, can't be his true self. It's hard to express yourself when your house is in ruins. But that, Jesus says, is what happens when we treat freedom like autonomy. We end up falling into patterns that keep us enslaved. What we need is Jesus's wisdom—His words—to shed clear light on our lives, revealing what's beautiful in us as well as showing us our brokenness.

How, exactly, does this work? What's the connection between Jesus's words and our becoming our truest, most electric selves? Over the years, I've found the following story from Brian Jay Jones's biography of the Muppeteer Jim Henson to be most illuminating, both for myself and in my work with deconstructing students and adults.

Before Jim Henson's Muppets had a film franchise, they had a sketch comedy show filmed in London (American studios weren't interested). Henson had been dreaming of creating *The Muppet Show,* so a lot was riding on the initial overseas filming. However, in his biography, Jones noted that as Henson's crew began to film *The Muppet Show,* most of the Muppet character skits were merely . . . fine. They had none of the electricity that made the Muppets come alive, and Henson knew it. Gonzo was a daredevil . . . so what? Miss Piggy was some kind of queen diva . . . but queen to whom? "Fozzie was a disaster," said Jerry Juhl, one of the writers. "It was embarrassing."[6] One week, Henson and his crew started to get impatient, having the strong sense that the skits weren't working. That was when he had an idea. He decided to throw one of his *Sesame Street* characters into the mix—the character that most represented Jim Henson himself: Kermit the Frog.

The moment Kermit came onstage, things began to sizzle.

After a sketch between Kermit and Fozzie Bear, Juhl said, "Suddenly Fozzie was *wonderful.* I remember that moment and saying, 'Now *there's* a character there!'"[7] Somehow the presence of Kermit helped all the characters *become themselves.* It was like they were all waking up from a long sleep. One intuitive critic of the show wrote that Kermit was "funny not because of what he does, but because of what others do around him, and because of the aplomb with which he bears their doings." Jones wrote,

[Kermit] was the sun around which the entire Muppet solar system revolved. "He relates to the other characters on many different levels," said Juhl. "More important, they *have* to relate to him. Without Kermit, they don't work. Nothing could happen without him. The other characters do not have what it takes to hold things together."[8]

Kermit brought out everyone's flavor. Their color. Their beauty. By becoming the central character in their story, Kermit liberated them to become themselves. Our relationship with Jesus is like that. He makes us who we truly are. We have to relate to Him. In the same way Jim Henson "sent himself" to be onstage with his Muppets, so the Father sent Jesus— and His Spirit—to be present with us that we might become our truest selves. That's because, without Jesus's wisdom, our world—our life—doesn't work. It crumbles, just like the HGTV house on the swamp. We just don't have what it takes to hold everything together. Jesus is the sun around which our entire solar system revolves. Kermit's wisdom is the key that unlocks the hearts of those surrounding him. In the same way, it's through Jesus's wisdom that He makes us our truest, freest selves. Jesus's words in Scripture are the DNA of creation. The sheet music of the world. The wisdom that brings freedom.

This is Jesus's second dream for you: That you might experience His freedom.

That you might embody that freedom in a community.

That you might extend that freedom to others.

EXPERIENCING JESUS'S FREEDOM: THE PRACTICE OF ANCESTRY

When I think of *experiencing* Jesus's freedom, I think of my friend Sajan.

Sajan reminds me of these words in T. S. Eliot's beautiful Ash Wednesday prayer: "Teach us to care and not to care / Teach us to sit still."[9] That's Sajan for you. Sajan has loads of wisdom. He'll courageously say what's true, but always gently. He comes across as someone with a deeply rooted perspective. It's what has enabled him to turn around some of the lowest-performing schools in America, build affordable workspaces for young artists and professionals, and become an effective leader at Praxis, an organization devoted to equipping Christian entrepreneurs to do meaningful good in society. This wisdom comes, in part, because although Sajan attends an evangelical church, he didn't grow up in the evangelical church. "My parents grew up in India, in the southern state of Kerala," Sajan said. "As Christians there, they were part of the Orthodox church. The Orthodox tradition emphasizes the historical origin of the church and how it would conduct worship services, which included the reciting of Scripture through a call-and-response set of liturgical chants issued from the priest from behind an altar. God's holiness was always on display and deeply honored, as were His designated leaders, the priests. Most of what we did has been followed by generations before us, dating back to the founding of the church."

This is what comes across to me in Sajan's personality: a sense of rootedness. A sense that he can gaze across the ages at you. A sense of ancestry. I didn't know it at the time, but this was also what attracted me to the faith of C. S. Lewis. Lewis is known for being a Christian intellectual. But I think what's truly attractive about Lewis, though we may not know it reading him, is that Lewis would really describe himself as a *medieval* Christian. When we read *Mere Christianity,* we're reading what Lewis called "the clean sea breeze of the centuries" blowing across its pages.[10] (He wrote those popular words, by the way, in his introduction to a classic ancient Christian text, Athanasius's *On the Incarnation.*) Lewis and Sajan never deconstructed their faith, because, for them,

Christianity was never something we moderns came up with in the first place. We can't deconstruct or reconstruct historic Christianity, because it doesn't belong to us. For them, the global, historic church—our Christian ancestors— deconstruct and reconstruct *us*.

Sajan immigrated to the United States after living in Canada for a few years.

These Canadian/Australian/U.S. church experiences emphasized a much more personal relationship with Jesus than I had encountered in my Orthodox experiences. They put a heavier emphasis on sermons and the intellectual processing of Scripture and small-group discipleship. These different worship experiences had a twofold effect on me. The first is it developed in me a love of liturgical worship—the sacraments, the common recital of ancient creeds, and the habitual progression and structure of a worship service. The second effect is that I love to be inspired, personally seen, and deeply moved through both song and word. My Eastern church upbringing gave me the first effect, and my Western church experiences the second.

Sajan has never been much interested in American Evangelicalism *or* American Progressivism. For him, these are strange little dots on the grand Christian horizon. Sajan's sense of ancestry—a faith shaped by the global, historic church instead of our limited cultural and sinful biases— gives him this perspective. This is why he's always settled into evangelical spaces that aren't interested in "Bully Church" culture. But he's also left spaces that at one time proclaimed faithfulness to orthodoxy but became beholden to American Progressivism. The wisdom of centuries of Christian thought empowered him to see through the shallowness of each of these American Christian subcultures.

The (formerly) progressive theologian Thomas Oden had a similar discovery late in life. Oden was a self-proclaimed "heretic who loved heresy" for the first forty years of his life. Then he was introduced to the idea of Christian ancestry.

> I did not become an orthodox believer or theologian until after I tried out most of the errors long rejected by Christianity. If my first forty years were spent hungering for meaning in life, the last forty have been spent in being fed. If the first forty were prodigal, the last forty have been a homecoming. . . .
>
> Every question I previously thought of as new and unprecedented, I found had already been much investigated. . . .
>
> As I worked my way through the beautiful, long-hidden texts of classic Christianity, I reemerged out of a maze to once again delight in the holy mysteries of the faith and the perennial dilemmas of fallen human existence. It was no longer me interpreting the texts but the texts interpreting me.[11]

This is how Oden describes his journey from a life beholden to the social gospel into a life spent rediscovering the church fathers and mothers. This kind of wisdom and perspective can be gained only when we embark on the lifelong journey of seeking out our Christian ancestry. Ancestry is about practicing what the early church called the "Rule of Faith": to seek out, learn from, and wholeheartedly affirm everything that has been believed by Christians "everywhere at all times." It's to continually ask the question, What did our ancestors say about this text? before offering up our own culturally captive ideas about what it could mean two thousand years removed from the sources. It's to let the light of the ages shed light on our own lives, freeing us from the shackles of our limited viewpoint. This means searching the Scriptures, of course . . . but not alone! We live in a village of people who've been thinking deeply and formatively about these scriptures for centuries. We'd be foolish to start from scratch. At a baseline, that means we need to be orthodox in our faith, making sure that what we believe about Scripture has survived the blood, sweat, and tears of the historic church. But adhering to the church's creeds, while very good, is the basement of ancestry, not the ceiling. To live out our ancestry, we need to delve into the riches of Christian thought that came before us, not simply to check the box of orthodoxy, but to truly experience and live out—alongside our brothers and sisters through the centuries—the liberating power of Jesus in our lives through the Scriptures. This isn't a box to be checked. It's a thrilling, lifelong adventure. As author Trevin Wax has put it in his wonderful book *The Thrill of Orthodoxy,*

> [Orthodoxy is] a map that doesn't require us to renounce our individuality and uniqueness, while also pointing us toward a path that's bigger than the one we'd choose for ourselves. . . .
>
> When someone says the adventure of life is in discovering or speaking *their* truth, it's like being enamored with the thermostat, excited to set the temperature that will produce the mild comfort of an air-conditioned home. The bigger adventure of orthodoxy calls us outside, away from the domesticated doctrines and palatable heresies of our time, and into a wild and glorious world of wonders.[12]

Reading the Scriptures alongside our colorful, ancient village of ancestors—this is how we experience the adventure of Jesus's freedom for each of us.

EMBODYING JESUS'S FREEDOM: THE PRACTICE
OF COVENANT

When I think of *embodying* Jesus's freedom, I think of my friend Emma. She shared,

> My faith was characterized by fear and pride in my childhood and well into adulthood. I confessed my sins and begged God to save me when I was six years old, motivated by fear of hell, judgment, failure, rejection, and a heavy sense that I wasn't good enough or doing enough for God. In my teenage years, an ironic shift occurred as my faith manifested as moralism and self-righteousness, judging others for their moral shortcomings according to all the boxes I was clearly checking as a dutiful Christian. In my twenties, I was introduced to Reformed theology, and though I was changed forever by the doctrine of grace, I also started stockpiling biblical knowledge and academic arrogance. Even into my early thirties, I held on to a belief that all the answers I was seeking were neat and tidy and safely within the box of my own religious experience and education.

Even as Emma grew in her head knowledge, there was a growing gap between the person she pretended to be and the reality of her life. In a radical turn of events, Emma—now the mother of three boys—was suddenly abandoned by her husband. "One year after my husband left, I began to pray that God would heal my heart so profoundly that I would be able to walk alongside other women with similar stories," she said. But this type of healing would need to go beyond academic knowledge of Scripture. Now, she realized more than ever, she needed a community where she could embody the wisdom she read about in the Scriptures.

"God knew I needed several sources of healing and renewal. Redeemer Presbyterian provided a safe place to land in the darkest days of my life. It provided Christian community that tangibly served as the hands and feet (and heart) of Christ when my kids and I needed them most. In addition, I spent a few years in counseling, unearthing cycles of hurt and dysfunction that I had no idea existed and countering the lies of ingrained shame and loneliness and worthlessness."

Over the years, I've been amazed to watch Emma be a loving, silly, and sometimes properly ferocious single mom to her boys, who've grown into godly, warm young men. But I've also seen the ways Jesus's wisdom has become embodied in her own story.

"When my world turned upside down," she told me, "I did not know anyone that could understand what I was going through, so I asked God to let me be that person for anyone that needed me. In these dark, heavy places, I have shared the light and hope of Christ, and I have relived trauma in the stories of others, but I know that God grants me the wisdom and strength to comfort others with the comfort He first provided to me."

Emma is articulating the freedom that can be found—freedom from bitterness, from trauma, from darkness—only in the wisdom of covenant community. To covenant is to promise faithfulness to another person or group. The reason covenant is so key to this community is simple: Covenant means our relationship isn't based on performance. In a society of transience, where "freedom" means jumping from one community or career opportunity to the next in order to self-actualize, the practice of covenant community—to live alongside others with all our quirks and foibles, in a specific geographical place where we can learn the cracks and crevices of things—is a radically countercultural way to embody the *true* freedom found in Jesus. How so? Think of Emma's story. Without covenant community, Emma's theological knowledge was like seeing the sun from inside a house. She was reading the Scriptures alongside her Christian ancestors, as described above. This is a beautiful thing. It's good to see the sun. But to be warmed and given life by it, you need to step outside, into the wisdom of covenant community: people who can speak the words of Scripture directly to you. Covenant community can encourage your particular personality, bear your particular burdens, and gently teach you in a way that suits your learning style. Acquiring theological knowledge without being in a community that encourages you, corrects you, rejoices with you, grieves with you, and ultimately loves you into Jesus's wisdom is like reading textbooks about health without visiting a doctor or shopping for clothes without ever looking in a mirror. To become your full self, you need others to apply Jesus's wisdom to your life. And *others need your voice as well.* Living in this covenant community is the true freedom Jesus offers to each of us. And it looks radically different from the freedom of self-actualization.

I recognize that if you've been hurt by a church community in the past, you're probably gun-shy about committing again. The great irony of being human is that we're most deeply scarred by relationships, but relationships are also our only way to heal from those scars. As someone who has my own scars, I'm telling you that covenantal relationships are the *only* way to experience renewal. Removing yourself from Christian community because you've been hurt is like avoiding the hospitals because you once had a bad doctor or never eating because you once had food poisoning. It's understandable, in a way, but it's also ultimately self-destructive. As pastor Tim Keller put it in his book *The Meaning of Marriage,* "To be loved but not known is comforting but superficial. To be known and not loved is our greatest fear. But to be fully known and truly loved is, well, a lot like being loved by God.

It is what we need more than anything."[13] That's covenant community.

Redeemer is a larger church that I tell people is constantly trying to grow smaller. We love our Sunday morning worship, but we recognize that having a covenant with such a large community isn't really a relationship. Sitting in the back of a worship room once a week isn't covenant community. Online streaming isn't covenant community. Podcasts aren't covenant community. Covenant community is a place where we're committed to one another and known by one another. As we seek to plant more neighborhood churches around the city (where community can be place-based and even walkable), we encourage folks to connect with their Redeemer neighbors through geographically based community groups. So even if Redeemer is too large to be my community, I still have a good, healthy-sized community of Redeemer friends in my neighborhood. Community groups help us get together. But they also, importantly, give us spaces to speak the truth in love to one another, and these are spaces where we help one another grow into our Christian freedom.

In my community group, I see Jesus's wisdom embodied in each of our members. Nick, a brand-new Christian, reminds me to look at the Bible with fresh eyes. Chris usually has some technical questions about Scripture he'd like me to answer, and I tell him I can't, but he reminds me to look at the Bible with a sharp mind. Liz keeps a prayer list and makes sure we check in with one another. She reminds me to think of the particular needs of people around me. Sarah brings the rawness, realness, and grittiness of life with her honesty in every meeting, and she reminds me that I can be my true, unguarded self before the cross of Jesus. Julianne tends to see the ways the Scriptures highlight justice and caring for others, and she pushes me to look hard at the parts that challenge my

American vision of life. Without the warmth of these other voices, I would simply read the Scriptures as a silhouette of me: my preferences, biases, and desires. But most of all, my covenant community reminds me that we're not in this life or this faith alone. We encourage one another. We shine the light of Jesus on the beauty we see in one another. We admonish one another. We tell one another when we see darkness.

And that allows each of us to become—slowly, painfully, beautifully—our truest self.

EXTENDING JESUS'S FREEDOM: THE PRACTICE OF WISDOM

When I think of *extending* Jesus's freedom, I think of my friend Ashley.

Ashley and her husband, Matt, both work in the medical field in Indianapolis. Matt works with underprivileged patients, and Ashley works in psychiatry, specifically caring for young adults with psychotic disorders.

"I feel very fortunate to say that in what I consider to be the most fundamental aspects of my faith, I continue to identify with the same beliefs that I grew up with," Ashley said. However, her upbringing also

> fostered a degree of skepticism, in particular toward many secular perspectives and fields of study. I gathered the impression that secular knowledge about the mind was at odds with Christian beliefs, and that science was not a valid tool for Christians to use to understand human thoughts, emotions, and behavior. The premise was that the Bible alone should be our authoritative source for both diagnosis and treatment of any kind of mental distress.

Most troublingly, there was sometimes a direct assertion that anyone experiencing either mental distress or mental illness was to blame for their own struggle, whether due to their lack of faith or unconfessed sin.

Let me press Pause here and describe what you're hearing. You're hearing a theology of escape manifesting itself through *exclusion*. Rather than believing Jesus is Lord over creation, in Ashley's story the Scriptures were pitted *against* creation, culture, and even our own bodies. In Ashley's description, you can hear the way we evangelicals often overspiritualize problems by assuming issues with the brain or body must actually be issues with the soul:

> In fact, when I began to tell people that I had decided to become a psychiatrist, a couple of close friends from my church staged an intervention with me to share their concern that I was denying the gospel by conceptualizing mental illness as anything other than the result of individual sin that should be addressed with prayer and Scripture. They were worried that I would lead people away from God by prescribing medication for mental illness. Even though I didn't believe this to be true, I myself had some reservations about whether or not psychiatry as a field might be incompatible with my faith. I wondered whether I might be guiding people away from Jesus by offering them nonreligious approaches to alleviate distress.

As Ashley read the Bible, however, she saw that the Scriptures themselves placed value on the things we learn from culture and creation. For instance, in a strangely detailed passage about how farmers use technology to create different spices, the prophet Isaiah proclaimed,

Caraway is not threshed with a sledge,
>   nor is the wheel of a cart rolled over cumin;
caraway is beaten out with a rod,
>   and cumin with a stick.
Grain must be ground to make bread;
>   so one does not go on threshing it forever.
The wheels of a threshing cart may be rolled over it,
>   but one does not use horses to grind grain.
All this also comes from the LORD Almighty,
>   whose plan is wonderful,
>   whose wisdom is magnificent. (28:27–29)

Isaiah said that all these little techniques for farming and creating spices in Middle Eastern culture *come from God.* In fact, he said that God "teaches" the farmer all these things (verse 26). How? Not through the Scriptures. Isaiah was speaking to the way God grants wisdom through human culture, specifically through the science of agriculture. God wants the farmer to see farming through the *lenses* of Scripture. But He wants him to look through those lenses to the *landscape* of the wide world around him. The same Augustine who had high praise for the Scriptures—"I have learned to yield this respect and honour only to the canonical books of Scripture: of these alone do I most firmly believe that the authors were completely free from error"[14]—also said these words against Christians who refuse to learn from the culture around them: "Wherever truth may be found, it belongs to [our] Master."[15] Augustine made special note of the way the Old Testament sayings in Proverbs, for instance, mostly come from Egyptian culture. Yet they are received, adapted, and then—to use philosopher Christopher Watkin's term—"out-narrated" by the authors of Scripture.[16] This out-narrating of the world is how we extend Jesus's wisdom—and therefore Jesus's freedom—to those around us.

To out-narrate the world means to see how every story the world is telling—in movies, in politics, in the language of our workplaces—fits into the larger story of Scripture. This is where the narrative of escape and the narrative of renewal take hugely different stances when it comes to Christians' engagement with the world. If the story of escape (sin, cross, disaster, rapture to heaven) is true, then the stories the world is telling have *nothing to do* with Jesus, since Jesus has nothing to do with earthly realities. This is why what we call evangelism is often complicated and manipulative. The gospel we're sharing with people has nothing to do with their lives, their deepest desires, their culture, or their needs. So the escapist evangelist needs to find complicated diagrams and tactics to get people interested. They load up with apologetic arguments to show how every single idea our non-Christian neighbor believes that's not directly from the Bible is false, wicked, and suspicious (again, something Augustine was battling against nearly two thousand years ago!). This is also why, oftentimes, escapist evangelicals feel that if something can be traced to a secular source, it can be disproven. So, for many evangelicals, if we can trace an idea to a secular philosopher or artist or politician, nothing more needs to be done. That means all we need to do is label something Marxist, woke, or postmodern, and voilà—we've done all the work we need to do.

But if the story of renewal (creation, fall, redemption, and new creation) is true, then *everything* in this world points back to Jesus. Within this framework, we can look at culture both graciously *and* critically. We can see God's goodness in the culture around us. But we can also see how the stories the world is trying to tell, absent of Jesus, are incomplete and self-destructive. As Christopher Watkin put it, "The danger of thinking in dichotomies and placing yourself on one side of them is that you become shaped by what you oppose and hate. . . . If your opponents are *for* something, then you must be *against* it; if they *reject* it, you must *embrace* it."[17] But the Christian doesn't need to do this. Rather than idolizing our viewpoints and demonizing others, we Christians can see how all viewpoints reflect the beauties of God's creation as well as the sinful realities of life . . . and how, ultimately, all these point to Jesus. The wisdom of out-narrating "is about telling the bigger story, the story within which all other stories find their place."[18]

One beautiful example of this is articulated in the book *How the Irish Saved Civilization* by Thomas Cahill. It's a book about Irish monks who were tasked with translating the Scriptures. Obviously, this was the heartbeat of what they did. But the Irish also saw it as their God-given task to preserve the books and literature of the Latin world, most of which we would not have today without them. It was *pagan* Europeans who saw no value in classical education. It was the *Christian monks* who saw God's fingerprints through it all.

> Wherever they went the Irish brought with them their books, many unseen in Europe for centuries and tied to their waists as signs of triumph, just as Irish heroes had once tied to their waists their enemies' heads. Wherever they went they brought their love of learning and their skills in bookmaking. In the bays and valleys of their exile, they reestablished literacy and breathed new life into the exhausted literary culture of Europe.[19]

So often, rather than wisely beautifying the worldviews around us as the Irish monks did, we evangelicals simply label different cultures or viewpoints "right" or "wrong," "Christian" or "non-Christian," "liberal" or "conservative." We make everything black and white in the name of truth. I can't tell you how many times I've witnessed this story:

A. Young evangelical starts to think maybe their progressive professor or friend has some insight.

B. Older evangelical tells the young evangelical their professor is a demonic Marxist.

C. Young evangelical determines that the older evangelical lacks wisdom and thus that Evangelicalism has been a blinded, tribal movement all along.

D. Younger evangelical becomes an exvangelical.

This entire narrative could be changed if we evangelicals could simply bring a little less exclusion and a little more light into our conversations about cultural issues.

At Redeemer, one way we cultivate the habit of out-narrating, or practicing wisdom, is a tradition started by our senior pastor and his wife, Charles and Erin Anderson, called "Gospel Optics." Friday night, once a month, we invite our high school upperclassmen to join us for games, free Tex-Mex, and a discussion about a hot cultural topic. That could be anything from school dances, the newest blockbuster film, a controversial article about social media, or Black Lives Matter. But it's the format we inherited from the Andersons that has taught our students the discipline of out-narrating. Rather than asking students whether they think what we're talking about is right or wrong, good or bad, we use the gospel story to frame our conversations:

1. Creation—How do we see evidence of God's wisdom, goodness, and beauty in the given viewpoint?

2. Fall—How does the perspective at hand show evidence that the world is broken?

3. Restoration—What are the deepest longings represented in this worldview, and how does Christ fulfill them?

It seems so simple. But it's truly profound, because the world knows how to think only in black and white. We're teaching these students how to think in color—to *out-narrate* the myopic hot takes they're surrounded by. By doing so, they'll bring light to everything they set their eyes and ears on. My hope is that my more progressive students could reasonably do this with their conservative friends: I hope they don't despise their MAGA friends but see the beauty, name the contradictions, and ultimately understand the heartache for Jesus's kingdom at the root of this vision. I hope my conservative students aren't disgusted with their friends with "secular creeds" posted on their front lawns—*Science Is Real, Black Lives Matter, No Human Is Illegal, Love Is Love, Women's Rights Are Human Rights,* and so on. I hope they can find the good in this vision, point out the fallenness, and show how it's ultimately a cry for Jesus's better, fuller dream of human flourishing (for a fantastic example of this kind of wise thinking, by the way, see Rebecca McLaughlin's wonderful book *The Secular Creed*).

One of the things I love to do is join friends at the local indie theater. My friend Nick became a Christian, in part, because we'd go to these little indie films together and discuss them. I'd tell him how I saw God's beauty in them, as well as the brokenness in the world. I'd tell him how these films pointed me to Jesus. I don't think Nick and I had one argument about Christianity. Because I believe Jesus is in the practice of renewing everything, I simply showed Nick where I thought Jesus was at work in his life—his circumstances, his artistic tastes, his deepest desires. When I recognized that the things he was hoping in—or idolizing—were leading to a dead end, I told him. To me, the best evangelists are people who (1) believe Jesus is at the center of everything, (2) have the intimacy with non-Christians to see where Jesus is at work in their lives, and (3) have the courage to name it. Eventually, Nick became curious about faith. As he put it to me recently, "Last year I was basically a pantheist. Right now I believe Jesus is God and He rose from the dead. If you told me last year I'd think that, I would have thought you were crazy. Sometimes I can't believe it myself, but here I am."

These conversations never would have happened in a minimall. Lots of folks from our church engage in groups like record clubs, creative writing groups, groups committed to the civic good of the neighborhood and city, or book clubs. Here, they quietly exercise the wisdom of Jesus by outnarrating the surrounding culture. They affirm the best of what's around them. They expose the brokenness in front of them. They are, one by one, helping our city become itself again. And often, as people trace the rays of their light to the source, people who don't know Jesus are led to the sunrise Himself.

That's Jesus's dream of freedom, coming true.

By the way, if this idea of out-narrating is new to you, it's something I try to model weekly at my Substack, *The Bard Owl* (www.substack.com/@thebardowl), where I offer weekly reviews and musings on both Christian and non-Christian books, movies, music, articles, and more.

12

Beauty

I want you to believe in things that you cannot.
—BRAM STOKER, *Dracula*

Roy Kent: That is not who I am I guess.
Ted Lasso: Not yet.
—*TED LASSO*

The first time I saw an evangelical displaying Jesus's radical beauty was when I met Big Steve. (Not to be confused with Musical Steve.) Big Steve was a pastor at a church in downtown Jackson, Mississippi. Big Steve's church, also called Redeemer, had moved into a low-income neighborhood a decade before, believing that since Jesus moved into a broken space, they should do that too. It soon became clear to Big Steve and others that the neighborhood's brokenness was a symptom of a larger problem: loan sharks. Before you get your hopes up, these are not the kind of sharks they make movies about who chomp on unsuspecting babes in front of their helpless boyfriends. Loan sharks provide short-term financial assistance to residents by offering loans for rent payments, but they charge high interest rates. Then they increase the price, bit by bit. This keeps residents stuck in terrible housing and unable to save for mortgages or to build wealth. The results? Economic hopelessness for them and their children. So

Redeemer began to purchase these houses from the neighborhood's landlords (slumlords), renovate them, and sell them back to the former tenants for affordable mortgages.

The effort required a village, so Big Steve was always recruiting skilled laborers (aka, youth group students) to help renovate. My church at the time in North Carolina was filled with them, so one summer we loaded our vans and made the ten-hour trek to Jackson. I was not a skilled laborer, but I went along. I tried to remember everything I'd learned at the builders' convention, but nothing came to mind other than the noogie. As the week progressed, I did become skilled at furrowing my brow and looking like I was concentrating on the house's infrastructure, when I was really thinking about how long I could wait before getting a third juice box without people getting angry and talking about me taking all the juice boxes.

A few days in, Big Steve noticed I wasn't doing anything, so he pulled me aside. He asked if I'd like to take my group on a prayer walk. "Sure!" I said. My introverted self wanted to hug Steve from a great distance.

Big Steve told me about all the great things that had happened on his prayer walks. He told how he broke up drug deals, shared his faith, and built relationships with people who he helped get jobs.

"Wait . . ." I said. "You actually *talk* to people on your prayer walks?"

"Well, yeah!" said Steve, smiling. "How else do you know what to pray for?"

"Oh, right," I said. "Of course."

I put on a brave face and told the group I was leading we'd now be going on a prayer walk. Then I quietly prayed that we would not see anybody. I told Jesus how I would get more praying done this way. On the walk, I wrote a little poem-prayer that went something like this:

Where are all the juice boxes?
They are nowhere on this prayer walk, Jesus.
Just think of that
Nowhere for me to slake my thirst.

We started down a neighborhood street, and then, to my horror, a young mom stepped out onto her porch. All the youth group kids looked to follow my lead.

"Hi," I started. *That's a thing people say, right? Hi?* "We're with the church down the street—"

"We know Redeemer," said the mother.

Uh-oh. Here we go.

Then she gave us a big, bright, warm smile. "We love that church!"

"Oh," I said. *She's a church member. Phew!* But it soon became clear the woman did not attend Redeemer Jackson. Yet, whenever she heard the church's name in our conversation, her eyes sparkled. House after house, it was the same story: single moms, kids, grown men . . . Most people smiled when we mentioned the church's name.

By the end of the week, I felt eager to tell people I was part of this special place.

Our last Sunday at Redeemer Jackson was a baptism Sunday. It was just after the Dallas shooting of several police officers by a veteran who was angry about police mistreatment of Black men. The takes on the issue, from Christians especially, were as discouraging as the event itself. The music that Sunday was an eclectic mix of old hymns, African spirituals, and praise. The lyrics were about Jesus's blood and atoning death, but they were also about real life. There was lament. There were cries for liberation from oppression. There was confession. People of different colors, ages, and classes were standing, singing, and clapping together in the pews.

The pastor that Sunday preached a sermon from a simple and beautiful scripture about Jesus as our priest. We celebrated the Lord's Supper together, but it was the baptism itself that struck me.

As the baptism portion of the service began, a family stood up onstage. The parents looked proudly on as the pastor took their baby in his hands and smiled and kissed him on the head. Tears filled my eyes.

After the service, I took a long walk through the streets of the neighborhood. I thought about what I'd just seen—a godly Black man caring for a little White baby in the midst of a country torn by racial tension.

As I walked, I said to myself, *That was the best sermon I've ever seen.*

These were Jesus's dreams of beauty, coming true.

STATUS VERSUS SERVICE

During college, I decided the whole Christian theology thing, and the whole church thing, was a huge cover-up to avoid doing what Jesus actually wanted us to do: serve the poor. When I read about His life, I was compelled by the beauty of it. Jesus's love for the poor and vulnerable felt like such a contrast to the ugliness I saw in the evangelical subculture. So I stopped going to church, and I tried to imitate Jesus with my life. I spent weekends feeding the homeless on Lower Wacker Drive in Chicago. I protested against child wars in Uganda. I gave guitar lessons to my classmates and donated all the proceeds to crisis pregnancy centers.

But I had two problems.

First, I never cared too much about the people I was feeding on Lower Wacker Drive, the kids in Uganda, or the charities I gave to. I felt numb about them. I did feel really good about *myself,* but for some reason, everything I was doing felt like zombie service. No heart. Just brains.

Second, I started to get angry with everyone who wasn't following Jesus like I was. *What a bunch of losers.* I treated them that way too. Anyone who wasn't on board with my radical agenda, to me, was a sorry excuse for a human being. I wanted to see a revolution. I wanted to see Jesus's kingdom, here and now, and no one was getting on board. And me, being me, often told them as much. So I didn't have many friends. I alienated my family members. The low-income folks I was working with weren't helping either. I was trying to fix their problems, and they weren't interested. But most importantly, I didn't allow anyone within an inch of who I really was. There was a reason for that: When I was being my most honest self, I had to admit the hollowness of my own heart.

I felt like Kitty from Leo Tolstoy's novel *Anna Karenina.* Kitty, a wealthy aristocrat, decided one day to emulate her pious friend by devoting herself to the poor. But a young painter weirdly confused her charity for flirtation, and she felt increasingly disgusted by the experience.

> She felt the whole dreariness of that world of sorrow, and of sick and dying people, in which she had been living; the efforts she had made to like it now seemed to her agonizing, and she longed to get away as soon as possible, to some fresh air.

Her body was serving the poor, but her heart wasn't in it. When the whole thing dramatically blew up in her face, she reflected,

> It serves me right because all of it was pretense, it was all made up, it didn't come from the heart. Why should I have

had anything to do with a stranger? . . . Pretense—
pretense! . . . The point was to seem better to people, to
myself, to God; to deceive anyone! No—I'll never give in to
that again! Even if I'm bad, at least I won't be a liar, a
fraud![1]

This is exactly how I felt about myself at the time. Everything I was doing was to appear better to people, myself,
God; to deceive everyone. I wasn't an SJW (social justice
warrior). I was an SJJ (social justice jerk). I longed for the
beauty of shalom. But my desire for status kept shooting my
good causes in the foot.

This hit home for me in one particularly ugly conversation.
I had just met my now wife, Brenna, who also worked with
low-income kids in downtown Kankakee, Illinois. Unlike me,
Brenna seemed to have a genuine affection for these kids.
She prayed for them, cried for them, and delighted in their
little quirks. So one day, casually, I mentioned to her that I
also was devoted to the poor. I told her how I was using some
of my monthly checks to support a kid in another country.

"But," I said, "he's kind of a tool. He used to draw me
pictures of gardens and his family. Now he just draws me
stupid little stick figures that say, 'Me.' Why isn't he more
grateful? What's the point of this 'school' I'm paying for? I
feel like his art is getting *worse,* not better."

Brenna looked at me like she could see the resounding hollowness that was the empty cave of my soul. "Where does he
live?"

". . . Internationally."

"What does that mean, exactly, *internationally*?"

"Internationally. You know, like, not *here.*"

"Right . . . You don't know where he lives, do you?"

"I mean, I couldn't pinpoint it on a map."

"So no. Okay. When was the last time you wrote him?"

"Wrote him? I don't know, it's been a busy six years. I haven't had time."

"What's his name?"

"It's in a different language, so you probably wouldn't be able to pronounce it since you're American."

"You're American too."

"Well—"

"You don't know his name, do you?"

Here I chose to let the glaring silence answer that question for me.

"And," she said, "you're surprised that he's making you stick figures now . . . *why*?" She was pointing to something in me I could barely name in myself: I was trying to create beauty in the world, but I didn't have the right tools to do it. Because of that, my acts of justice and service were subtle acts of trying to gain status. When people didn't respect me or get on board or show their eternal gratitude, I was finished with them. It's something I saw regularly, later on, in my progressive students at the University of Missouri. There was an apocalyptic fervor to what they said, and if you weren't on board, they were going to go postal on you.

It's something the musician Nick Cave—certainly no conservative or Christian by any stretch—recently wrote about in his observations of the world today:

> Political correctness has grown to become the unhappiest religion in the world. Its once honourable attempt to re-imagine our society in a more equitable way now embodies all the worst aspects that religion has to offer (and none of the beauty)—moral certainty and self-righteousness shorn even of the capacity for redemption. It has become quite literally, bad religion run amuck.[2]

Cave agrees with the goals of the social justice agenda. Yet he's seeing the way it's giving rise to more and more SJJs like I was. What's happening here? Looking back, I see that I was trying to create the beautiful kingdom Jesus promised to us. I think that was good. But what I didn't understand was how or when it would come about. As Mark Sayers said of this generation, we're looking for the kingdom of God but without the King.[3] Without Christ as the author and definer of justice, justice becomes a nice word for *vengeance* for the vulnerable. It even becomes a word that excuses *self-indulgence* and *status* for the privileged. But with the hopeful perspective of Jesus's resurrection, His dreams fulfilled on the earth, and the final judgment, we become people who are free to serve.

HOW EVERYTHING BECOMES BEAUTIFUL AGAIN

This is the final movement, the *crescendo,* of Zechariah's song:

> You, my child, will be called a prophet of the Most High;
> for you will go on before the Lord to prepare the
> way for him,
> to give his people the knowledge of salvation
> through the forgiveness of their sins,
> because of the tender mercy of our God,
> by which the rising sun will come to us from heaven
> to shine on those living in darkness
> and in the shadow of death,
> *to guide our feet into the path of peace.* (Luke 1:76–79)

Notice everything coming to a head here. Everything Zechariah is singing about will lead to this purpose clause: "to guide our feet into the path of peace." We talked a few chapters ago about this idea of peace as the transcendent harmony of all things. Shalom. Maybe that sounds lovely to you, the way that never-never land sounds lovely. So let's get more specific by looking at Zechariah's Old Testament name-sake, the prophet Zechariah. We'll call him Retro Zechariah.

Retro Zechariah promises that the Messiah will create a beautiful world:

> On that day the LORD their God will save them,
>   as the flock of his people;
> for like the jewels of a crown
>   they shall shine on his land.
> For how great is his goodness, and how great his beauty!
>   Grain shall make the young men flourish,
>   and new wine the young women. (Zechariah 9:16–
>   17, ESV)

That's shalom. Harmony between all things, with Jesus at the center. Light. True beauty. But how will this come about? Retro Zechariah shows us:

> Behold, your king is coming to you;
>   righteous and having salvation is he . . .
>   and he shall speak peace to the nations;
> his rule shall be from sea to sea,
>   and from the River to the ends of the earth. (Zecha-
>   riah 9:9–10, ESV)

So the Messiah will come as a righteous king, and He will bring "peace to the nations." The Old Testament describes the Messiah as a king because the king, in the Hebrew imag-ination, is the person who brings *righteousness* and *justice* to the world. The king was not only in right relationship with God and others (righteousness). The king also had the power to right wronged relationships through justice. The poor, oppressed, and vulnerable, through the Messiah King, would have an advocate. This is why the most common way the Old Testament authors talk about the coming Messiah is this: He is the righteous and just king who brings shalom. "Righteousness and justice are the *foundation* of your throne," wrote the psalmist of the coming Messiah (Psalm 89:14). The coming Messiah is "righteous" (*tsadiq* in Hebrew)—He is in right relationship. And He is "just" (*mishpat*)—He will make wronged relationships right. Both of these must happen before we can have a beautiful world of shalom.

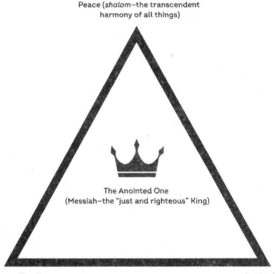

Peace (*shalom*–the transcendent harmony of all things)

The Anointed One
(Messiah–the "just and righteous" King)

Righteousness (*tsadiq*–
right relationships with
God and one another)

Justice (*mishpat*–
righting wronged
relationships)

But how will the Messiah bring about this righteousness and justice? Retro Zechariah already showed us. Jesus's justice will be reflected in *His people's lives,* "for like the jewels of a crown *they shall shine on his land*" (Zechariah 9:16, ESV). Notice that people will see the greatness of King Jesus's beautiful justice as they *see us reflecting that beautiful justice.* This is why when Zechariah the priest sings about peace, he doesn't say, "Bring peace to us eventually." He says Jesus will lead *us* "into the path of peace." We the church are meant to be Jesus's arms of righteousness and justice in the world around us. Look at how Isaiah put it:

> Is not this the kind of fasting I have chosen:
> to loose the chains of injustice
>   and untie the cords of the yoke,
> to set the oppressed free
>   and break every yoke?
> Is it not to share your food with the hungry
>   and to provide the poor wanderer with shelter—
> when you see the naked, to clothe them,
>   and not to turn away from your own flesh and
>   blood?
> Then your light will break forth like the dawn,
>   and your healing will quickly appear;
> then your righteousness will go before you,
>   and the glory of the LORD will be your rear guard.
>   (58:6–8)

Isaiah was saying to God's people that only when our faith comes to its crescendo in a life of advocacy for the poor will we reflect the light of King Jesus. King Jesus will heal the world and make it beautiful once again, through us. That's what it means to walk in the path of peace.

RESURRECTED KINGDOM

There's one more thing to notice about Retro Zechariah's prophecy. Notice *how* the righteous king brings justice and peace to the world:

See, your king comes to you,
> righteous and victorious,
lowly and riding on a donkey,
> on a colt, the foal of a donkey.
I will take away the chariots from Ephraim
> and the warhorses from Jerusalem,
> and the battle bow will be broken. (Zechariah 9:9–10)

Jesus will establish His justice, yes, but He won't do it with the weapons of this world. Tools for warfare can restrain evil, but they can never create shalom. Rather, Jesus will establish His justice in the strangest way possible. He will set up His righteous and just kingdom . . . by being humbled, even humiliated.

He comes riding on a donkey.

Jesus is showing us that His kingdom isn't going to come through people consumed by *status*—whether it's political, religious, or economic. His kingdom will come through people who *serve*. Think about it. If Jesus never rose from the dead, we wouldn't likely know anything about His life of humble service. When Jesus was offered a crown of status, He denied it (John 6:15). Instead, He said He will establish His kingdom in a most unexpected way: "Very truly I tell you, unless a kernel of wheat falls to the ground and dies, it remains only a single seed. But if it dies, it produces many seeds" (John 12:24). The righteous kingdom of Jesus will come about through humility, through service, through His own death. Riding on a donkey is nothing remarkable. Making carpentry for thirty years, serving the poor, and then being crucified like a common criminal outside the city doesn't sound glorious. But in light of Jesus's resurrection, we can see it *was* glorious. All of it.

This is what I was missing in college. I didn't know what time I was in. I didn't understand that the beauty of Jesus's kingdom will only, *finally,* come through Jesus's future return. Jesus will come again, not on a donkey, but on a warhorse in the final judgment, when He fully establishes His shalom throughout the world (Revelation 19:11–16). That may sound harsh to our ears. But this was exactly my problem in college: I had stripped *my* version of Jesus of any wrath or judgment. As a result, *I* had to take His place. Since my Jesus had no wrath, I was full of wrath. Since my limp Jesus would never come in judgment, I felt the need to strong-arm everyone around me. In his book *Dominion,* agnostic historian Tom Holland notes that the reason the French Revolution was full of so much needless, senseless bloodshed was simply this: The French Revolutionaries were atheists. They didn't believe in God's judgment. Because of that,

> as the spring of 1794 turned to summer, so [the guillotine] blade came to hiss ever more relentlessly, and the puddles of blood to spill ever more widely across the cobblestones. It was not individuals who stood condemned, but entire classes. Aristocrats, moderates, counter-revolutionaries of every stripe: all were enemies of the people. To show them mercy was a crime. . . . The only heaven was the heaven fashioned by revolutionaries on earth. Human rights needed no God to define them. Virtue was its own reward.[4]

I hope we shudder at these words. This is not the justice we're looking for. We need a Christ of judgment. We need a

Christ of resurrection. We can't be people who walk in the path of peace without the King of Peace.

There is a very liberating side to all this. What I didn't understand in college was that to follow Jesus as King, you have to be a person of *hope*. The first time Brenna and I could afford to see the musical *Hamilton* was the day it came out on Disney+ for $9.99. That weekend, Brenna and I watched the performance together in our basement. I had just read Ron Chernow's humongo and incredible biography of Hamilton, so I came prepared. As we watched, both of us found ourselves identifying with the characters. I felt some kinship with Hamilton, who was filled with passion and fury about injustice but whose emotional intelligence was lacking. He furiously tried to "write his way out" of every circumstance—his affair, his political rivalries, his poverty and orphanhood—but he simply couldn't.

I got the impression he was the kind of person it would be fun to tease.

Brenna related to Eliza, Hamilton's wife, who watched him: "He will never be satisfied." She believed in Hamilton's ideals. Yet she saw the way the story he was telling himself just wasn't working. His ego and self-consumption were handicapping what were, truthfully, his brilliant plans for American economics, the freeing of slaves, and the American political system. But he was so obsessed with "not giving away his shot" at success, he smothered the people and situations around him with a flood of ideas and arguments, shooting his grand plans in the foot.

The key plot of the musical is Hamilton's rivalry with Aaron Burr. Burr didn't care about justice, and Hamilton despised him. After much back and forth, the climax of the play—which was true to life—was Aaron Burr's challenging of Hamilton to a duel.

Now, what was clear in Chernow's biography was that

Hamilton's long-suffering, patient, and incredibly gifted wife Eliza was a devout Christian. And years before Burr's challenge, Hamilton himself was converted to her faith. Things began to change. We sensed those changes most clearly in Hamilton's final gun duel with Burr. Hamilton—an excellent marksman who would have relished the chance to take down his rival a decade before—raised his pistol in the air . . . in surrender. A man obsessed with "not throwing away his shot" did just that: He threw away his shot at vengeance.

Then . . . Burr shot him.

Hours later, Hamilton was served his last communion and died peacefully the following morning after uttering the words, "I am a sinner. I look to His mercy. . . . I have a tender reliance on the mercy of the Almighty, through the merits of the Lord Jesus Christ."[5]

But the story didn't end there. Hamilton's humble death, strangely, made his work all the more effective, as his wife, Eliza, accomplished so much of what he dreamed about: the founding of an orphanage, the work of abolition, the establishment of an equitable economic system.

Here is the way I see it. Without Jesus, Hamilton was trying to change the world in his lifetime. He needed justice *now*. But his egotism—his desperation for status—shot all his beautiful ambitions in the foot. But the story of Jesus gave Hamilton *hope*. He saw that even if he didn't make the world beautiful in his lifetime, Jesus would use whatever seeds he planted to bring beauty in His own time. Because Jesus promised to judge the world in the future, Hamilton was freed from judging his wayward neighbor, Aaron Burr. This freed Hamilton to pursue his vision as a humble servant, not as a status seeker. And, ironically, it's that act of self-sacrifice that spurred Hamilton's dreams into the realities we see today.

This is Jesus's dream of beauty, coming true.

This is Jesus's final dream for you: That you might experience His beauty.

That you might embody that beauty in a community.

That you might extend that beauty to others.

EXPERIENCING JESUS'S BEAUTY: THE PRACTICE OF SEASONAL PRAYER

When I think of *experiencing* Jesus's beauty, I think of my artist friend Kyle.

Kyle grew up in what he calls "a sweet southern church."

"It was very relational. Not harsh. But I did grow up with a performance-based, maybe more religious, understanding of 'be good, try hard, work hard, show you love Jesus.' That worked awesome for me for thirty years, I think. I was a Young Life leader, super involved, served really hard, loved it." And it did work. Kyle was leading several outwardly successful ministries. "God was doing all these great things, and I was experiencing worship like I never had, and the youth ministry was going well. When my pastor called me to do youth ministry, I felt like God was calling me, like that was the right thing to do."

Then, one day, everything collapsed. "The church was very wealthy, and the pastor didn't play the political games correctly. He was beloved by lots of people, but he was all of a sudden taken out. And it was so weird and unbelievable and anti anything good. I was so disappointed. I felt at the time like God had brought me there just to emotionally slaughter me. I felt like I had given my whole life for this thing just for it all to be blown up."

After seeing the way politics and wealth had crept in and destroyed his local church, Kyle, understandably, could have given up on church altogether. But as it happened, Kyle was also a gifted up-and-coming artist in Indianapolis, living in the basement of Redeemer.

When I asked him about Redeemer, he laughed. "I'm not going to say what you think I'm going to say," he told me.

I told him to say it anyway.

"I hated Redeemer. Hated it. I hated the music. It was very uptight. Very rigid."

I asked him why he came.

"I lived in the building, so it was easy to go to the church." Over time, however, Kyle did notice something different about Redeemer. There was a spirit that was different. A tone. Over his years of faithfulness, he began to understand what that was. "Coming here, I recognized the difference of the gospel—that God already loves you; you don't have to perform in order for Him to approve of you. It made so much more sense. Then life can be hard . . . and God still be good."

Today Kyle is one of the most well-known artists in Indianapolis. Pretty much anywhere you turn, you'll see a Kyle Ragsdale mural or commission. But one of the things most people in Indianapolis don't see is the way Kyle has faithfully led our liturgical arts team at Redeemer. In a surprising twist, God began to use Kyle's gifts in art and in ministry, and "all my background started to come together." Kyle was living in the basement of Redeemer in the first place because of a woman named Joanna Taft. Joanna herself had gone through a faith transformation over the years, especially in the way she thought about Jesus bringing beauty to the world. As she told me, "I grew up in a Presbyterian church in the Reformed tradition, strong on doctrine but weak on social concern." Yet, as a member of Redeemer's fledgling church plant, Joanna found herself launched into a career in the arts. That's because when our old, dilapidated building in the heart of downtown was sold to us in Redeemer's early years, it just so happened to be a place where several artists were also renting studios. Rather than kicking them out in order to make space for our church, a new dream was born: What if our church building was *also* a place where we could continue to show hospitality to artists in the city, no matter their faith background? What if we could continue to bring beauty to our downtown community in a way the *community itself* was asking for? This wasn't on the church-planting bingo card. But in that moment, it became part of Redeemer's vision, and under Joanna's leadership, the Harrison Center for artists launched alongside Sunday morning services at Redeemer. Kyle was one such artist.

Over the years, I've seen God heal people's hearts and lives through Joanna's work at the Harrison Center and Kyle's work with the liturgical arts team. Joanna speaks for so many of us when she says, "Experiencing beauty in a community setting reweaves my doubt and discouragement into faith. Beauty calls me to worship and lifts my heart to marvel at God's power. It's the best apologetic." Sometimes artists can say things in stark and disruptive ways. That's hard. It's also good for us. "Art," Joanna says, "helps reveal what is really going on in our hearts." When you walk into Redeemer, you won't find the kind of art you'll find in Christian bookstores. You'll see things that captivate you with beauty and things that repel you and make you shudder. But this beautifully disorienting work has been so formative and helpful for many of us, especially those of us who feel wounded by the church. Just last week, someone shared with me how the first time they walked into Redeemer's sanctuary, they knew they were in a space for healing from past church hurt. There is a kind of retro-future vibe to the whole thing: a century-old sanctuary adorned with projects from artists young and old.

But at the heart of our sanctuary art is a centuries-old

Christian practice: the practice of seasonal prayer. From the very earliest days of the church, practicing seasonal readings and prayers was a way to recognize that creation itself told the story of Jesus. So the liturgical calendar is a way to recognize how the seasons God has created reflect the very life, death, and resurrection of Jesus Himself. It's no coincidence that Easter—part of the church calendar most of us celebrate—is in the spring. Springtime itself is a way the beauty of creation is connected to the beauty of Jesus. But there is so much more here. That's why Kyle and his team of composers, graphic novelists, painters, florists, carpenters, and crafters of all kinds help us follow the ancient tradition of living out the gospel story through the liturgical calendar all year long, from Advent to Easter to Ordinary Time. For example, during Advent—the part of the year when we celebrate Jesus's coming to earth—we began to teach about how Jesus was fully human. The result? A gigantic church window modeled after a multilayered, multicolored, microscopic view of human skin. Wooden sculptures of human DNA springing out of logs. A crocheted X-ray of a woman's pregnant body. The liturgical arts team doesn't hold back. We don't ask them to. They're basically the Willy Wonkas of church. And yes, their art is beautiful and magical. But it's all helping our church experience Jesus's beauty. I've found living through Jesus's story every year, alongside the global church, incredibly enriching. Easter Sunday isn't one moment on the calendar for us. It's a day of explosive joy and feasting because the whole liturgical year has led up to this moment. Lent begins with an Ash Wednesday service, where we cling to one another in solemn prayer that often lasts well into the night. While my kids look forward to gifts on Christmas, they also know it's the time when we read, sing, and remember the holy beauty of Jesus's life on earth. As I look around our sanctuary, filled with bones and strange woodwork, I see the glory of Jesus's servant-kingship.

"I feel like in the past thirty years people have less capacity to pay attention," says Kyle. "It's almost like we're going back to the Middle Ages. So as you think about the Middle Ages, visual things impacted religious congregations. I strongly believe in the liturgical calendar shaping us slowly over time. The art and the color and the mood and different times of year shape us as people. And what we see around us as we're worshipping impacts what we're hearing, how we're reacting."

How can you begin to experience the beauty of Jesus? Start by practicing seasonal prayer. The most common starting place for this is the Book of Common Prayer, the first version of which was completed in 1549 by a man named Thomas Cranmer. Cranmer had a vision to craft a book of prayers and scriptures that met three standards: It needed to be ancient ("agreeable to the Word of God and the primitive Church"[6]), universal (as Alan Jacobs put it, Cranmer "retained some of the most venerable and beautiful aspects of traditional worship but also fully embodied the evangelical commitment to serious engagement with Scripture"[7]), and understandable for everyone (John Wesley, no high liturgist, wrote, "I believe there is no liturgy in the world, either in ancient or modern language, which breathes more a solid, scriptural, rational piety, than the Common Prayer of the Church of England"[8]). Today the Book of Common Prayer is used by Christians all over the world, "as far from England as South Africa, Singapore, and New Zealand."[9] Even if you don't have wonky art adorning your sanctuary walls on Sundays, you can still participate in the beauty of the church calendar as you pray through the Book of Common Prayer or some other seasonal readings.

You don't need professional artists to creatively participate either. As Kyle told me, "You could follow the church calendar with simple decorations in your house—on your table or in your living room—that represent Lent or Eastertide." Over time, the sights, sounds, smells, touch, and taste of these things will bring a healing experience of Jesus's beauty to your life. I'd also add, if you want to participate in seasonal prayer, step outside. I often wonder how much of our secularized culture comes from our insulation, where we control the temperature and the paint colors and order all our food from a grocery store directly to our homes. Tribal cultures aren't atheistic. It's not because they're uneducated. It's because they're deeply educated in the ways the earth actually works: times, seasons, plants, elements. They each have a sense that a beautiful King is out there, calling to them. So maybe the best thing you can do for faith renewal is pick up the Book of Common Prayer, or a simpler version of it. (Here at Redeemer, we love Joel Littlepage and Ashley Williams's resource, the Daily Prayer Project, which incorporates contemporary global songs and prayers as well.)[10] If you're new to reading Scripture or if reading Scripture by yourself feels too complicated because of church wounds, just start with the psalm of the day. Walk around for fifteen minutes outside, reflecting on it and responding to it. It's okay. You don't need to do more than that. As you pray and explore, you'll begin to *experience* the beauty of Jesus.

EMBODYING JESUS'S BEAUTY: THE PRACTICE OF PARTNERSHIPS

When I think of *embodying* Jesus's beauty, I think of my wife, Brenna.

Brenna, like me, has had to untangle her fair share of evangelical culture from her faith. A gifted artist who, as a high school student, quickly received recognition from teachers and attention from colleges, she hasn't always felt at home in American evangelical culture. Brenna has a deep appreciation for music, literature, and visual art that doesn't blink at the bleakness of life. That often meant she felt mismatched with the plastic, happy-clappy nature of the American evangelical world. However, Brenna was fortunate to belong to a church and a family that taught her one clear way to face into the ugliness of reality as well as create beauty in Jesus's name: by partnering with others to care for the vulnerable. Brenna has taught me, over the years, that in order to bring the beauty of Jesus to the spaces around us, we need to be people who embody it ourselves. To this day, she outruns me in her gut-felt compassion, her dogged commitment to the vulnerable, and her unfettered delight in the down-and-out. I see that in the way she cares for our own children and our home. I also see it in her work at the Oaks Academy in downtown Indianapolis.

Some weeks ago, Brenna and I were at the post office. It was Christmastime, so a tough season for postal workers. The younger woman helping us seemed down until she learned where Brenna worked. She looked up at my wife with a warm, beautiful smile.

"You work at the Oaks?" she said. "I just sent my daughter to pre-K there. We love it."

That's because the Oaks is unlike any school I've ever seen. It's a private school, but an important part of its mission is to provide a stellar education to low-income families. As of now, 40 percent of the students are White, 40 percent are Black, and 20 percent are Hispanic, Asian, or multiracial. Most impressive to me, though, is that 25 percent of the students are considered high income, 25 percent middle income, and 50 percent low income.[11] Brenna will tell you that makes for interesting, wild, and sometimes heartbreaking classroom sessions. She works as the building sub as well as at the front desk, so she needs to know the name of every student, in every classroom, every day. It's an incredibly difficult job, but she loves it (most of the time). She gets to be with kids of all backgrounds. She's helped students dealing with family homicides, panic attacks, and racist comments from other students. The Oaks isn't heaven on earth. Yet the majority of the students who begin in poverty are finding healing at the Oaks—generational healing. After generations of wealth being stripped from our minority students' families through slavery and segregation, the Oaks is providing healing where it's most effective: through childhood education. It's not coming from a government program (though government programs have actually been a huge blessing to the Oaks!). It's coming from Christians from all backgrounds, uniting to heal what's broken in our country and in our city. It's motivated not by vengeance, anger, or self-righteousness but by a heartfelt belief that Jesus is a just and righteous king who wants us to embody His vision of beauty by practicing the way of peace in our neighborhood, together.

So, what would it look like for you and me to embody Jesus's servant-kingship day in and day out? It looks like engaging in partnership. By "partnership," I mean joining with other Christians—in America, especially, this needs to happen between Black and White Christians—to serve the cause of justice (*mishpat,* or "right-making") in your community. That will mean, in some measure, getting political. And while some people criticize evangelicals for being too political, I think what they mean is this: We evangelicals are often engaged in politics in order to preserve our status, not to serve others. Being political is part of loving our neighbors, especially those disadvantaged by the law. The problem is, in our racially and economically homogenous political echo chambers, we can't possibly fulfill Paul's command to imitate Jesus in this way: "Do nothing out of selfish ambition or vain conceit. Rather, in humility value others above yourselves, not looking to your own interests but each of you to the interests of the others" (Philippians 2:3–4). When Paul said we are to look to, or consider, the needs of others, he wasn't saying we should sit around by ourselves and wonder what other people might need and take that into consideration. He was talking about deep, heartfelt listening to the priorities of Christians outside our bubble.

When I talk about justice in my evangelical circles, some of my conservative friends get twitchy. They say, "You should just preach the gospel" or "You're being too political" or "You're teaching the social gospel." They write me angry letters saying they're canceling their support for my ministry because I'm a flaming liberal who's betrayed the very foundations of our country and the Constitution, which was written by Jesus Himself, and I should just go be a social worker and shut up about the poor and hungry and destitute and, by the way, they hope I die in a giant pit of a thousand burning eels. If eels can even burn. I could say all kinds of things to these accusations, like the fact that this critique makes no sense since the social gospel movement was actually a short-lived initiative whose heresy was denying our personal need for the atonement of Jesus, and I wrote a whole book about how we each need the atonement of Jesus (called *Faker*).

But I won't say that.

Instead, let me make a personal appeal. So very often, when older evangelicals ask what they can do to prevent deconstruction, here's what I say: "If you want to do one single thing that will help your niece, grandson, or children see

Christianity as credible, it's this: Form a bridge where the world can't. Sit down with your minority Christian brothers and sisters, and model the gospel of reconciliation. Stop reading about 'them.' Stop assuming things. Partner with them. Have hard conversations. Do good together in your community. Tell your niece or grandson or children what you're learning and how you're growing in Christ through these conversations. There are millions of young people waiting to see the power of the gospel. They want to see it. Until they do, none of your apologetic seminars matter. For the next generation, witnessing the gospel at work in the world *is* the apologetic. If they don't see this in your life, they're going to look for it elsewhere."

That's when people usually tuck their wallets away. But not always. Sometimes people listen. Sometimes people change. I'm one of those people. I'm still in process. I'm still changing. Years ago, I was extremely skeptical of my minority brothers and sisters in Christ. I may not have said that out loud, but because of my entirely White background, natural biases and hostilities had formed in my heart. It's been through knowing, listening to, and seeing the image of God in my minority brothers and sisters over the years that God has gradually changed my perspective. So yes, I believe Jesus can—and will—do that in the life of our evangelical church. He's doing it in my life. He's doing it in the life of our city. He can do it in our evangelical community and bring His servant beauty to the world.

EXTENDING JESUS'S BEAUTY: THE PRACTICE OF SERVICE

When I think of *extending* Jesus's beauty, I think of my friend Erin.

Erin is someone I admire because of the way she's able to

see so many facets of life in light of Jesus's beauty. She's committed to her vocation as a mother and truly sees this as central to her calling by Jesus (and that's looked different over the years!). She's also a professor at a reputable secular university here in Indianapolis, stewarding her intellectual and professional gifts. And finally, she brings care, life, and creativity as she serves our church.

Which of these things, for Erin, is a true extension of Jesus's beauty? All of them. But she hasn't always felt that way.

"How can I be an accountant and actually take my faith seriously?" she asked herself on her college graduation day. "Don't accountants just want to get rich and steal from people? We've all read the story of Zacchaeus the tax collector—wasn't he basically an accountant? Feeling that my chosen major and career choice were less Christian was a recurring thought for me as, one by one, my like-minded peers felt the 'call' to various ministry fields. Their call to ministry left me feeling like I must be less spiritually mature, not as serious about my faith."

As Erin entered grad school, her worst fears seemed to be confirmed. "I learned that Zacchaeus really would have fit in among my colleagues. No, they weren't trying to steal from people, but most were driven by a sense of personal gain. Many nights on the train home, as a self-identified Enneagram 3, I contemplated a career change—one that would be more rewarding, not necessarily to me, but to the Christian world I wanted badly to fit into." It wasn't until Erin encountered the gospel as a story of *restoration*—not a story of escape—that she began to see Jesus might just care about her "secular" work as much as He cared about her friends' "spiritual" work.

"I was introduced to the big storyline of the Bible," she shared. "That Sunday school class changed my view of my career and calling and, by extension, my life and hopefully others' along the way. It was during this one-hour class on Sunday mornings that I began to fight the whole secular/sacred split and realize that all professions participate in the goodness of creation, are distorted by sin, and can be cultivated toward beauty in Christ's redemption. I now had a more biblical and life-giving framework for my work."

What does that mean, exactly, for Erin? It means she sees her nine-to-five work as a professor and accountant as an act of *service*, not as a way to increase her status. And it really does make a difference in how she does her work.

> Greedy corporate executives manipulating data for their own personal gain reminds me that my sin and the sins of others have fueled the growing belief that no organization or person is to be trusted. Auditors get to do ministry by helping a client find unintentional errors and restoring investor confidence. Work that was once mundane to me has now taken on new meaning. Every day as an auditor, I get to live out the creation-fall-redemption drama. My work as a certified public accountant is part of cultivating the earth, and that matters to God.

Erin's service, especially to the vulnerable, is Jesus bringing beauty to the institutions she serves in. She also extends Jesus's beauty in the way she teaches college students, who will often spend hours in her office talking not only about accounting but also about life. They sense Erin is living from a different story both in the way she teaches and in the way she frames the work they're being called to do.

"I don't use gospel words," she says. "But my hope is that my students see something different in my classroom that is contagious and that they will want to explore these truths and the bigger story they fit in, long after their final grade is posted."

How can you and I extend Jesus's servant-kingship each day?

We begin by seeing all our work—both at home and in the workforce—as acts of service. I mean "service" in the broad, ancient Hebrew sense of the term. In fact, the Old Testament Hebrew word for "work," describing the calling of Adam and Eve ("to work [the ground] and keep it"[12]), is also the word for "serve": "to serve the ground and keep it" (or, less archaically, "protect it"). Cultivating the garden so it yielded a beautiful harvest, then establishing civilizations filled with cities and culture and life, was how Adam and Eve would "serve" the earth. So we serve in our work when we beautify the world around us. We also serve in our work when we keep (or protect) the vulnerable from harm. As the Scriptures continue, this vision unfolds: If the world is God's temple, then as we make it beautiful, we are preparing it for His presence to come, in the era of shalom. *This* is a reason to get out of bed in the morning. It's a reason to do the dishes. It's a reason to care for your email inbox (or not!). If it's true that Jesus wants to bring His servant-kingship to bear on all of creation, then *every moment of your day matters.* I invite you to pause and take an inventory of all the things Jesus has called you to cultivate in your life right now. I think you'll find He has given you far more responsibility than you realize.

Simple acts of service done in Jesus's name are far more profound than radical acts done to draw attention to ourselves. And if Jesus is really telling a story of restoration, that means He cares about bringing healing to everything your hands touch. How could your day look different if you really believed that to be true? For me, it's made all the difference in the world. When I struggle to believe my day or my life matters or when I feel down or depressed, I try to remember the words of Paul: "Make it your ambition to lead a quiet life: You should mind your own business and work with your hands, just as we told you, so that your daily life may win the respect of outsiders and so that you will not be dependent on anybody" (1 Thessalonians 4:11–12). My work doesn't have to be loud. It can be quiet and done with love. I can reflect the beauty of Jesus when I do my work, not to achieve status in this life, but to serve others. Great chefs will tell you that everyone can subconsciously taste the difference in a meal made with love. Serving through your work in Jesus's name might not look radical on the outside, but the difference is what's inside: It's done with love. And that makes all the difference.

The English missionary Lesslie Newbigin, after spending forty years in India, returned to England in the 1970s and found a very different country awaiting him: It was no longer essentially Christian. It had secularized. Yet, Newbigin noted, churches and Christians were still acting as though they lived in a Christian country. They were acting like everyone was ready to hear the gospel message, with no preparation. Newbigin, as a missionary, argued otherwise. In a non-Christian culture, the gospel needs to be demonstrated in our lives and communities before anyone has interest in its content. In the West, he said, that means the first place we will demonstrate the gospel is *in our public life.*[13] If you sincerely create beauty, protect the vulnerable, and serve from the heart in all your work, you're preparing the way for Jesus to enter someone's life. Before our neighbors understand the truth of Jesus, they need to see the beauty of Jesus. People must be enchanted before they're convinced. We show that beauty, not through acts of greatness or dominance, but through small, humble, everyday acts of service.

In one of his famous letters, Martin Luther wrote to a cloister of monks who believed their vocation was truly God's work, whereas other people's vocations weren't as important. Luther asked them whether they believed God had provided their milk and meat. Of course they did. But how? "God milks the cows," he wrote, "through the vocation of the milk-maid."[14] Through her vocation, the milkmaid cultivated creation around her. In doing so, she was extending Jesus's beauty. If Jesus isn't merely helping us escape the world but is renewing all things, then every act of service we do in His name will echo into eternity. That's why, when Paul finished his long argument for a physical resurrection (the Corinthians wanted to overspiritualize the resurrection), he concluded his remarks with these simple words: "In the Lord your labor is not in vain" (1 Corinthians 15:58, ESV).

That's true because someday Jesus's dream of beauty will come true. Inasmuch as you and I extend that beauty through service, we proclaim and participate in His dream.

Benediction

Many people of all ages and classes and of both sexes are now being enticed. . . . The superstition has spread like the plague, not only in the cities but in the villages and the countryside as well.

—PLINY THE YOUNGER ON THE SPREAD OF
CHRISTIANITY, A.D. 112

Almost the greater part of the world is now committed to this truth, even whole cities.

—LUCIAN THE MARTYR, A.D. 350

After Zechariah sang his prayer, he exited stage left, never to be seen or heard from again. At least not in Luke's narrative. But I don't think Zechariah was offended, because his name means "remember." The angel called Zechariah to remember God's dreams. As Zechariah pondered in his season of silence, he remembered the story of God, and he was re-storied. Restored.

Zechariah was restored by God's story, and that story includes us all.

One day after the January 6 insurrection, Tish Harrison Warren wrote,

Wednesday January 6 was the Feast of Epiphany, when Christians celebrate how the light of Christ spreads to all nations. . . . But what a strange Epiphany we had in the United States. . . . Instead of the baptism of Christ announcing his true identity, men and women held signs proclaiming "JESUS SAVES" as they demanded to overturn an election. . . . Light is beautiful, and it is also revelatory. . . .

It exposes darkness. And the church must reckon with the "unfruitful works of darkness" (Eph. 5:11, ESV) that this anti-epiphany—and all that has led to it—makes visible.[1]

Warren's point is profound. Epiphany was meant to be a celebration of the church as a light to the nations. But on January 6, Jesus chose to shed light on *us*. Why? The same reason He always sheds light on things: to transform them. To make us the people we're meant to be. To re-create us. To renew us. To restore us.

During the insurrection, I heard a news reporter ask, "Is this the end of something? Or the beginning of something?"[2]

I didn't know then. But now I believe the answer is up to us. January 6 could be the end of Evangelicalism's long downward spiral over the past century. But it could also be a beginning. Because here's a secret about this book: Nothing I've written is new. These three ministries of Christ—as our Priest of love, Prophet of freedom, and King of beauty—are central to the vision of the ancient church. They're clearly articulated in the gospel set out in the Westminster Confession of Faith, finalized in 1648.[3] The Puritan Thomas Boston went so far as to say any gospel that excludes one of these ministries of Christ is no gospel at all.[4] The early church spoke about these three roles as the fulfillment of everything promised in the Old Testament.[5] And when the church was spreading like wildfire in the first through third centuries, pagans were in awe of the ways Christians exercised hospitality, wisdom, and service toward the people around them.

Writing in the early fourth century, the pagan politician King Julian (yup) complained that the church was multiplying like rabbits around him, but note what he observed in their behavior: "The impious Galileans [Christians], in addition to their own, support also ours, [and] it is shameful that our poor should be wanting our aid."[6] He also wrote, "Why then do we . . . not observe how the kindness of Christians to strangers, their care for the burial of their dead, and the sobriety of their lifestyle has done the most to advance their cause?"[7]

Do you hear it?

Kindness to strangers—hospitality.

Sober lifestyle—wisdom.

Support for the poor—service.

Would that this were the complaint from politicians about us today!

But this vision goes even further back. Listen closely to Luke's description of the earliest church:

> They devoted themselves to the apostles' teaching and to fellowship, to the breaking of bread and to prayer. Everyone was filled with awe at the many wonders and signs performed by the apostles. All the believers were together and had everything in common. They sold property and possessions to give to anyone who had need. Every day they continued to meet together in the temple courts. They broke bread in their homes and ate together with glad and sincere hearts, praising God and enjoying the favor of all the people. And the Lord added to their number daily those who were being saved. (Acts 2:42–47)

Here was a church glowing with light. They were practicing hospitality, both inside and outside the church. They were exercising wisdom. They were engaging in service. As they experienced, embodied, and extended Jesus's kingdom in their neighborhoods, they were Jesus's dreams, coming true.

And so are we.

We *are* Jesus's kingdom experienced, embodied, and extended.

We *are* people of hospitality.

We *are* people of wisdom.

We *are* people of service.

We *are* the dreams of Jesus, coming true. Jesus's plan is to bring love, beauty, and freedom into the world through us. We're plan A. There is no plan B. So, as Paul wrote to the church over and over again, go be who you already are, in Christ.

Go be the people Zechariah sang about:

> You, my child, will be called a prophet of the Most High;
>> for you will go on before the Lord to prepare the
>>> way for him,
> to give his people the knowledge of salvation
>> through the forgiveness of their sins,
> because of the tender mercy of our God,
>> by which the rising sun will come to us from heaven
> to shine on those living in darkness
>> and in the shadow of death,
>> to guide our feet into the path of peace. (Luke
>>> 1:76–79)

When we experience, extend, and embody Jesus's dreams of love, beauty, and freedom, the nations *will* flock to Jesus. How do I know this? Not because I'm an optimist. I know this because God promised it will happen:

> I, the LORD, have called you in righteousness;
>> I will take hold of your hand.

I will keep you and will make you
    to be a covenant for the people
    and a light for the Gentiles,
to open eyes that are blind,
    to free captives from prison
    and to release from the dungeon
        those who sit in darkness. (Isaiah 42:6–7)

The words sound familiar, don't they? They're the words Jesus uses to talk about *us:* "You are the light of the world. A town built on a hill cannot be hidden" (Matthew 5:14).

Acknowledgments

All books are community projects. This book is no different.

My first thank-you is, and always will be, to my wife, Brenna. You are responsible, more than anyone, for the renewal of my faith. I saw the light in your eyes, and I followed you into it.

> And in my wanderings I did meet
> Another searching too:
> The dawning hope, the shared quest
> Our thoughts together drew;
> Fearless she laid her hand in mine
> Because her heart was true.[1]

Thank you to my RUF friends and mentors, who showed me the meaning of grace. Thanks especially to Michael Gordon, who continually showed me firmness and grace. Thanks to Chris Horne ("Cool Chris"), who welcomed me in with open arms. Thanks to Justin Smith for your little green book.

Thank you to my church, Redeemer, for giving me space and time for this project and for showing me what it means to live it out. Thanks especially to Charles Anderson for valuing this project because of your passionate care for God's broader kingdom.

Thank you to the good folks at Redeemer Jackson for your faithfulness, your hope, and your work in the Lord. Thank you for speaking the truth in love to me. Thank you for showing the truth in love to me.

Thank you to Austin Wilson, my agent. You saw this random project in your email inbox and decided to believe in it. I admire your integrity. It truly gives me hope.

Thank you to Estee, my editor, and to Multnomah and others who made this project so much better and more beautiful. You took a risk on this project because you believed in its vision. I'll be forever grateful to you for that. Estee, you've helped this project become itself, and you never lost sight of the people this project is meant to serve. Thank you.

Thank you to everyone who shared your insight into the earliest versions of this book.

Thank you to my mom, Kim McDonald. You were the first person who taught me to dream. I wouldn't be who I am today without the light in your eyes and your passing it on to me.

To Dave Mann, Caleb Keitt, Sarah Miller, and Craig Miller. Thanks for taking the time to shape this project to be more helpful to readers everywhere.

Thank you to Trevin Wax for your encouragement, time, and helpful insights into this book. Thanks especially for widening my vision of hope to extend beyond my tribe.

Thanks to my late grandma Karen, who passed away as this book was being written. You made it possible for me to go off to England and chase a dream.

Thank you to my professors at Gordon-Conwell, specifically Rick Lints. You all gave me the grander vision for Evangelicalism I didn't know I didn't have. You gave me the tools to find renewal in the Scriptures.

Thank you to two men who were patient and wise partners in my faith renewal: Steve Weibley and Kirk Blankenship.

Thank you to everyone who has allowed your story to be part of the story I'm telling in this book.

To Caleb, Owen, and Russell. You've endured way too many hours of Daddy making edits, being in a brain fog, and being caught up in my own world as I created this project. You've always been patient and kind and curious about it. I love you more than words can say. I hope this book is a gift to you someday.

Notes

FOREWORD

1. Alister McGrath, "The State of the Church Before the Reformation," *Modern Reformation,* March 1, 1995, www.modernreformation.org/resources/articles/the-state-of-the-church-before-the-reformation.
2. McGrath, "State of the Church."
3. McGrath, "State of the Church."

CHAPTER 1: Disillusionment, Deconstruction, and the Great Dechurching

The second epigraph is from the blog *Of Is & Was,* July 3, 2023, https://ofisandwas.substack.com/p/both-the-wicked-and-the-righteous?utm_source=publication-search.

1. Jim Davis and Michael Graham, *The Great Dechurching: Who's Leaving, Why Are They Going, and What Will It Take to Bring Them Back?* (Grand Rapids, Mich.: Zondervan Reflective, 2023), 5.
2. Lecrae (@lecrae), "Many don't realize there have been healthy Deconstructions throughout history that have lead to health," Twitter (now X), September 14, 2022, 8:31 A.M., https://x.com/lecrae/status/1570057600607076360; Lecrae (@lecrae), "Many movements from the reformation to the civil rights movement involved deconstruction," Twitter (now X), September 14, 2022, 8:31 A.M., https://x.com/lecrae/status/1570057604734537736.
3. Alisa Childers and Tim Barnett, *The Deconstruction of Christianity:*

What It Is, Why It's Destructive, and How to Respond (Carol Stream, Ill.: Tyndale, 2023), 26.

4. Davis and Graham, *Great Dechurching,* 27.

5. Thomas S. Kidd, *Who Is an Evangelical? The History of a Movement in Crisis* (New Haven, Conn.: Yale University Press), 19, Kindle.

6. John Dickson, quoted in Tim Alberta, *The Kingdom, the Power, and the Glory: American Evangelicals in an Age of Extremism* (New York: Harper, 2023), 128.

7. John Stackhouse, "What Is Evangelicalism? An Interview with John Stackhouse," interview by Michael Bird, Early Christian History with Michael Bird, video, 32:03, January 14, 2022, www .youtube.com/watch?v=DUn649-O15I.

8. Kathryn Stelmach Artuso, "Defamiliarize, Don't Deconstruct: Reconsidering Contemporary Christian Trends," Mockingbird, July 23, 2024, https://mbird.com/philosophy/defamiliarize-dont-deconstruct -reconsidering-contemporary-christian-trends.

9. Michael Rosen and Helen Oxenbury, *We're Going on a Bear Hunt* (New York: Little Simon, 1997).

10. Davis and Graham, *The Great Dechurching,* 27.

11. Dickson, quoted in Alberta, *The Kingdom, the Power, and the Glory,* 139.

12. "Break on Through (to the Other Side)," The Doors, track 1 on *Perception,* https://genius.com/The-doors-break-on-through-to-the -other-side-lyrics.

CHAPTER 2: Deconstructing

1. Andrew L. Seidel, "Christian Nationalism and the Capitol Insurrection," Select Committee to Investigate the January 6th Attack on the United States Capitol, U.S. House of Representatives, March 18, 2022, www.govinfo.gov/content/pkg/GPO-J6-DOC -CTRL0000062431/pdf/GPO-J6-DOC-CTRL0000062431.pdf, 17; Emma Green, "A Christian Insurrection," *Atlantic,* January 8, 2021, www.theatlantic.com/politics/archive/2021/01/evangelicals -catholics-jericho-march-capitol/617591.

2. "The Name Philippi," Abarim Publications, www.abarim-publications .com/Meaning/Philippi.html.

3. Jim Davis and Michael Graham, *The Great Dechurching: Who's Leaving, Why Are They Going, and What Will It Take to Bring Them Back?* (Grand Rapids, Mich.: Zondervan Reflective, 2023), 10.

4. Davis and Graham, *The Great Dechurching,* 10.

5. Luke Simon, "Who Was 'i' Without My iPhone?," The Gospel Coalition, September 2, 2024, www.thegospelcoalition.org/article /i-without-iphone.

6. David Brooks, "America Is Having a Moral Convulsion," *Atlantic,* October 5, 2020, www.theatlantic.com/ideas/archive/2020/10 /collapsing-levels-trust-are-devastating-america/616581.

7. Brian Little, "Who Are You, Really? The Puzzle of Personality," TED, February 2016, www.ted.com/talks/brian_little_who_are_you _really_the_puzzle_of_personality.

CHAPTER 3: Exclusion

1. Esau McCaulley, *Reading While Black: African American Biblical Interpretation as an Exercise in Hope* (Downers Grove, Ill.: Inter-Varsity Academic, 2020), 91, 8 (emphasis mine).

CHAPTER 4: Relevance

1. Ben Sixsmith, "The Sad Irony of Celebrity Pastors," *The Spectator World,* December 6, 2020, https://thespectator.com/topic/sad -irony-celebrity-pastors-carl-lentz-hillsong (italics in the original).

2. Charles Marsh, *Strange Glory: A Life of Dietrich Bonhoeffer* (New York: Vintage Books, 2015), 103.

3. *Merriam-Webster,* s.v. "pragmatism (*n.*)," accessed September 1, 2024, www.merriam-webster.com/dictionary/pragmatism.

4. Reggie L. Williams, *Bonhoeffer's Black Jesus: Harlem Renaissance Theology and an Ethic of Resistance,* rev. ed. (Waco, Tex.: Baylor University Press, 2021), chap. 1, Kindle.

CHAPTER 5: Vacuum

1. Nicholas T. McDonald, *Faker: How to Live for Real When You're Tempted to Fake It* (Epsom, UK: Good Book, 2015).

2. C. S. Lewis, "The Weight of Glory," in *The Weight of Glory: And Other Addresses* (New York: HarperOne, 2001), 29–31.

3. C. S. Lewis, "Is Theology Poetry?," in *The Weight of Glory: And Other Addresses* (New York: HarperOne, 2001), 140.

4. Exodus 3:7–8.

5. Genesis 12:1–3.

CHAPTER 6: Escape

1. Richard F. Lovelace, *Dynamics of Spiritual Life: An Evangelical Theology of Renewal* (Downers Grove, Ill.: InterVarsity, 2020), 376.
2. Andrew Wilson, *Remaking the World: How 1776 Created the Post-Christian West* (Wheaton, Ill.: Crossway, 2023), 309.
3. Karen Swallow Prior, *The Evangelical Imagination: How Stories, Images, and Metaphors Created a Culture in Crisis* (Grand Rapids, Mich.: Brazos, 2023), 136.
4. J. N. Darby, quoted in Crawford Gribben, *J. N. Darby and the Roots of Dispensationalism* (New York: Oxford University Press, 2024), 70.
5. Gribben, *J. N. Darby,* 119.
6. Gribben, *J. N. Darby,* 63.
7. Gribben, *J. N. Darby,* 154.
8. Daniel Hummel, *The Rise and Fall of Dispensationalism: How the Evangelical Battle over the End Times Shaped a Nation* (Grand Rapids, Mich.: William B. Eerdmans, 2023), 88.
9. Helen Howarth Lemmel, "Turn Your Eyes Upon Jesus," 1922, Hymnary.org, https://hymnary.org/text/o_soul_are_you_wear_and _troubled.
10. Dietrich Bonhoeffer, *The Cost of Discipleship* (New York: Touchstone, 1995), 45.
11. D. L. Moody, quoted in Lovelace, *Dynamics of Spiritual Life,* 377.
12. Lovelace, *Dynamics of Spiritual Life,* 377.
13. Lovelace, *Dynamics of Spiritual Life,* 377.
14. Marko Marina, "Marcion (and Marcionism): The Untold Story of an Early Christian Heresy," Bart Ehrman, June 27, 2024, www .bartehrman.com/marcion.
15. Polycarp, "Epistle to the Philippians," chapter 7, https://ccel.org /ccel/polycarp/epistle_to_the_philippians/anf01.iv.ii.vii.html.
16. Tertullian, *The Five Books Against Marcion,* trans. Peter Holmes, in *Ante-Nicene Fathers,* vol. 3, *Latin Christianity: Its Founder, Tertullian,* ed. Allan Menzies (Edinburgh: T&T Clark, n.d.), www.ccel .org/ccel/schaff/anf03.v.iv.ii.xxiv.html.
17. Augustine, *On Christian Teaching,* trans. R. P. H. Green (Oxford: Oxford University Press, 1997), 16.

CHAPTER 7: Re-storied

1. Oscar Wilde, quoted in Richard Ellmann, *Oscar Wilde* (New York: Vintage Books, 1988), 581.

2. Charles Dickens, *A Christmas Carol and Other Christmas Books* (New York: Oxford University Press, 2006), 23.
3. Ecclesiastes 1:2, 18; 2:4–15; 3:11; 12:13–14.
4. Billie Eilish, "What Was I Made For?," Billie Eilish and Finneas O'Connell, July 13, 2023, YouTube video, www.youtube.com/watch?v=cW8VLC9nnTo.
5. Paul Borthwick, *Western Christians in Global Mission: What's the Role of the North American Church?* (Downers Grove, Ill.: Inter-Varsity, 2012), loc. 334, 356, Kindle.
6. Lamin Sanneh, *Whose Religion Is Christianity? The Gospel Beyond the West* (Grand Rapids, Mich: William B. Eerdmans, 2003), 43.
7. Matthew 23:23.
8. Matthew 22:29.
9. John 10:35, ESV.
10. Matthew 22:43.
11. Matthew 5:18.
12. Matthew 19:29.

CHAPTER 8: Zechariah

1. C. S. Lewis, "The Weight of Glory," in *The Weight of Glory: And Other Addresses* (New York: HarperOne, 2001), 26.

CHAPTER 9: Shalom

1. *The Beatles: Get Back,* directed by Peter Jackson, aired November 25, 2021, on Disney+.
2. C. S. Lewis, "The Weight of Glory," in *The Weight of Glory: And Other Addresses* (New York: HarperOne, 2001), 42.
3. Craig Foster, *Amphibious Soul: Finding the Wild in a Tame World* (New York: HarperOne, 2024), 7.
4. C. S. Lewis, *The Collected Letters of C. S. Lewis,* vol. 1, *Family Letters: 1905–1931,* ed. Walter Hooper (San Francisco: Harper-SanFrancisco, 2004), 976–77.
5. "He recommended Isaiah the Prophet; I believe, because he above the rest is a more clear foreshower of the Gospel and of the calling of the Gentiles." Augustine, *Confessions,* ed. William G. T. Shedd (Andover, Mass.: Warren F. Draper, 1860), 218.
6. Steven McKinion and Thomas Oden, eds., *Ancient Christian Commentary on Scripture, Old Testament X, Isaiah 1–39* (Downers Grove, Ill.: InterVarsity, 2004).

7. J.R.R. Tolkien, *The Silmarillion* (New York: HarperCollins), loc. 5, Kindle.

8. Tolkien, *Silmarillion,* loc. 5.

CHAPTER 10: Love

1. Freddie deBoer, "Selfishness and Therapy Culture," *Freddie deBoer,* Substack, July 31, 2024, https://freddiedeboer.substack.com /p/selfishness-and-therapy-culture?utm_source=publication -search.

2. "Birdman or (The Unexpected Virtue of Ignorance): Quotes," IMDb, accessed November 8, 2024, www.imdb.com/title/tt2562232 /quotes.

3. "4698—splanchna," Bible Apps by Bible Hub, accessed December 18, 2024, https://bibleapps.com/strongs/greek/4698.htm.

4. *Pig,* directed by Michael Sarnoski (Los Angeles: Pulse Films, 2021).

5. Justo L. González, *The Story of Christianity,* vol. 1, *The Early Church to the Reformation,* rev. ed. (New York: HarperOne, 2010), 59–60.

6. Acts 2:42–47.

7. Heidelberg Catechism, Question 75, in Lyle D. Bierma, *The Theology of the Heidelberg Catechism: A Reformation Synthesis* (Louisville, Ky.: Westminster John Knox, 2013), 167.

8. Redeemer Presbyterian Church, "Confession," October 1, 2023, https://static1.squarespace.com/static/5aec630e3e2d0934d11 d88ae/t/65170215206b5175edf99f8b/1696006678123/RPC -Print+10-01-2023.pdf.

9. "Strong's G5381—Philoxenia," Blue Letter Bible, accessed November 8, 2024, www.blueletterbible.org/lexicon/g5381/kjv/tr/0-1.

CHAPTER 11: Freedom

1. "Washington's Dream," Saturday Night Live, video, 4:50, October 29, 2023, www.youtube.com/watch?v=JYqfVE-fykk.

2. Jemar Tisby, "The Patriotic Witness of Black Christians" in "Christian Nationalism and the January 6, 2021, Insurrection," https:// static1.squarespace.com/static/5cfea0017239e10001cd9639/t /6203f007e07275503964ab4d/1644425230442/Christian _Nationalism_and_the_Jan6_Insurrection-2-9-22.pdf.

3. See Plato's *Phaedrus* for a popular conception of this.

4. Steve Martin, *Born Standing Up: A Comic's Life* (New York: Scribner, 2007).

5. Christopher Nolan, "Memento Explanation by Christopher Nolan," interview by Vikas Thippani, video, 17:53, August 21, 2015, www .youtube.com/watch?v=67e_jl4flpE.

6. Brian Jay Jones, *Jim Henson: The Biography* (New York: Ballantine Books, 2016), 235.

7. Jones, *Jim Henson,* 244.

8. Jones, *Jim Henson,* 244.

9. T. S. Eliot, *Ash-Wednesday,* in *The Poems of T. S. Eliot,* vol. 1, *Collected and Uncollected Poems,* ed. Christopher Ricks and Jim McCue (London: Faber & Faber, 2015), 88.

10. C. S. Lewis, preface to Athanasius, *On the Incarnation, Credo,* July 22, 2022, https://credomag.com/2022/07/preface-to-on-the -incarnation-by-c-s-lewis.

11. Thomas C. Oden, *A Change of Heart: A Personal and Theological Memoir* (Downers Grove, Ill.: InterVarsity, 2014), 56–57, 138–39.

12. Trevin Wax, *The Thrill of Orthodoxy: Rediscovering the Adventure of Christian Faith* (Downers Grove, Ill.: InterVarsity, 2022), 37, 39–40.

13. Timothy Keller and Kathy Keller, *The Meaning of Marriage: Facing the Complexities of Commitment with the Wisdom of God* (New York: Penguin Books, 2016), 9.

14. Augustine, letter 82, in *A Select Library of the Nicene and Post-Nicene Fathers of the Christian Church,* ed. Philip Schaff, vol. 1, *The Confessions and Letters of St. Augustin, with a Sketch of His Life and Work* (Buffalo, N.Y.: Christian Literature, 1886), 350.

15. Augustine, *On Christian Doctrine,* trans. J. F. Shaw, in *The Works of Aurelius Augustine,* vol. 9, *On Christian Doctrine; The Enchiridion; On Catechising; and On Faith and the Creed* (Edinburgh: T. & T. Clark, 1873), 55.

16. Christopher Watkin, *Biblical Critical Theory: How the Bible's Unfolding Story Makes Sense of Modern Life and Culture* (Grand Rapids, Mich.: Zondervan Academic, 2022), 21–22.

17. Watkin, *Biblical Critical Theory,* 21–22 (italics in the original).

18. Watkin, *Biblical Critical Theory,* 21.

19. Thomas Cahill, *How the Irish Saved Civilization: The Untold Story of Ireland's Heroic Role from the Fall of Rome to the Rise of Medieval Europe* (New York: Anchor Books, 1996), 196.

CHAPTER 12: Beauty

1. Leo Tolstoy, *Anna Karenina,* trans. Constance Garnett (McAllister Editions, 2015), 184.
2. Nick Cave, "What Is Mercy for You?," The Red Hand Files, August 2020, www.theredhandfiles.com/what-is-mercy-for-you.
3. Mark Sayers, *Disappearing Church: From Cultural Relevance to Gospel Resilience* (Chicago: Moody, 2016), 80.
4. Tom Holland, *Dominion: How the Christian Revolution Remade the World* (New York: Basic Books, 2019), 404–5.
5. Ron Chernow, *Alexander Hamilton* (New York: Penguin, 2004), 708.
6. Act of Uniformity, 1552, quoted in Alan Jacobs, *The Book of Common Prayer: A Biography* (Princeton, N.J.: Princeton University Press, 2013), 50.
7. Jacobs, *Book of Common Prayer,* 54.
8. John Wesley, quoted in Jacobs, *Book of Common Prayer,* 54.
9. Jacobs, *Book of Common Prayer,* 5.
10. Daily Prayer Project, accessed November 10, 2024, www.dailyprayer project.com.
11. "School Profile," The Oaks Academy, accessed November 9, 2024, www.theoaksacademy.org/school-profile.
12. Genesis 2:15, ESV.
13. Lesslie Newbigin, "Can the West Be Converted?," *International Bulletin of Missionary Research* 11, no. 1 (January 1987): 2–7; Timothy Keller, *Center Church: Doing Balanced, Gospel-Centered Ministry in Your City* (Grand Rapids, Mich.: Zondervan, 2012), 252–54.
14. Martin Luther, *Luther's Works,* vol. 21, *The Sermon on the Mount (Sermons) and the Magnificat,* ed. Jaroslav Pelikan (St. Louis, Mo.: Concordia, 1958), 237.

BENEDICTION

The first epigraph quote is from "Pliny, *Letters* 10.96–97," https:// faculty.georgetown.edu/jod/texts/pliny.html.

The second epigraph quote is from Rodney Stark, *Cities of God: The Real Story of How Christianity Became an Urban Movement and Conquered Rome* (New York: HarperOne, 2006), 64.

1. Tish Harrison Warren, "We Worship with the Magi, Not MAGA," *Christianity Today,* January 7, 2021, www.christianitytoday.com

/ct/2021/january-web-only/trump-capitol-mob-election-politics
-magi-not-maga.html.

2. Tom Jones, "CNN's Van Jones: 'We Don't Know What We're
Looking at Yet. Is This the End of Something? Or the Beginning
of Something?,'" Poynter, January 6, 2021, www.poynter.org
/commentary/2021/cnns-van-jones-we-dont-know-what-were
-looking-at-yet-is-this-the-end-of-something-or-the-beginning-of
-something.

3. Westminster Shorter Catechism, Question 23.

4. Thomas Boston, *The Offices of Christ* (Louisville, Ky.: Vintage Puritan, 2017), 8.

5. Eusebius, *The Church History of Eusebius,* trans. and ed. Arthur
Cushman McGiffert, in *A Select Library of the Nicene and Post-
Nicene Fathers of the Christian Church,* ed. Philip Schaff and
Henry Wace, vol. 1, *Eusebius Pamphilus: Church History; Life of
Constantine; Oration in Praise of Constantine* (Edinburgh: T&T
Clark, 1890), www.ccel.org/ccel/schaff/npnf201.iii.vi.iii.html.

6. Julian, letter to Arsacius, in Joseph Cullen Ayer, Jr., *A Source Book
for Ancient Church History: From the Apostolic Age to the Close of
the Conciliar Period* (New York: Charles Scribner's Sons, 1922),
333.

7. Julian, letter to Arsacius, Louisiana Tech University Department of
History, accessed November 9, 2024, www2.latech.edu/~bmagee
/201/swinburn/Julian.html.

ACKNOWLEDGMENTS

1. George MacDonald, *Discovering the Character of God,* ed. Michael Phillips (Minneapolis: Bethany House, 1989), 20–21.

ABOUT THE AUTHOR

NICHOLAS MCDONALD is an assistant pastor at Redeemer Presbyterian Church in central Indianapolis and has served in ministry for more than fifteen years. His previous positions have included roles in youth ministry and four years as the campus minister of Reformed University Fellowship at the University of Missouri. McDonald received his MDiv from Gordon-Conwell Theological Seminary, studied film at Olivet Nazarene University, and studied creative writing at Oxford University. He writes regularly through his Substack, *The Bard Owl,* and is also the author of *Faker.* He lives in Indianapolis with his wife and their three children.